COUNTING
THE
COST

COUNTING
THE
COST

JILL DUGGAR

WITH DERICK DILLARD AND CRAIG BORLASE

GALLERY BOOKS

New York   London   Toronto   Sydney   New Delhi

G

Gallery Books
An Imprint of Simon & Schuster, Inc.
1230 Avenue of the Americas
New York, NY 10020

First Gallery Books hardcover edition September 2023

GALLERY BOOKS and colophon are registered trademarks of Simon & Schuster, Inc.

For information about special discounts for bulk purchases, please contact Simon & Schuster Special Sales at 1-866-506-1949 or business@simonandschuster.com.

The Simon & Schuster Speakers Bureau can bring authors to your live event. For more information or to book an event, contact the Simon & Schuster Speakers Bureau at 1-866-248-3049 or visit our website at www.simonspeakers.com.

Interior design by Jaime Putorti

Printed and bound by CPI Group (UK) Ltd, Croydon CR0 4YY

10 9 8 7 6 5 4 3

Library of Congress Cataloging-in-Publication Data has been applied for.

ISBN 978-1-6680-2444-7
ISBN 978-1-6680-2446-1 (ebook)

To those who have been harmed in the name of "religion."
To those who have suffered behind closed doors and have yet to
find their voice.

To those who have begun to find their voice but may still be living
in a season of isolation.

To those who like Esther of the Old Testament Bible story have
courageously answered the call for *"such a time as this"*
(Esther 4:14), and despite the backlash have now found their voice.

From victims and survivors, to strangers, family, and friends,
this book is dedicated to you. May you all know
that you are not alone. That your story, your voice,
and your mental health matter.

The Lord is a stronghold for the oppressed,
a stronghold in times of trouble.
—Psalm 9:9 ESV

CONTENTS

FAMILY TREE

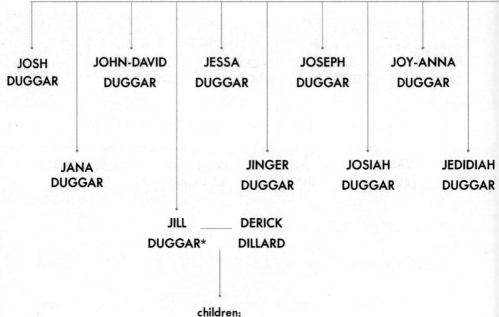

JIM BOB
DUGGAR

JOSH
DUGGAR

JOHN-DAVID
DUGGAR

JESSA
DUGGAR

JOSEPH
DUGGAR

JOY-ANNA
DUGGAR

JANA
DUGGAR

JINGER
DUGGAR

JOSIAH
DUGGAR

JEDIDIAH
DUGGAR

JILL ——— DERICK
DUGGAR* DILLARD

children:
Israel, Samuel, and Freddy

MICHELLE DUGGAR
(NEE RUARK)

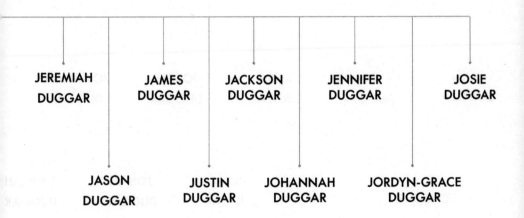

JEREMIAH
DUGGAR

JAMES
DUGGAR

JACKSON
DUGGAR

JENNIFER
DUGGAR

JOSIE
DUGGAR

JASON
DUGGAR

JUSTIN
DUGGAR

JOHANNAH
DUGGAR

JORDYN-GRACE
DUGGAR

COUNTING
THE
COST

For which of you, intending to build a tower, sitteth not down first, and counteth the cost, whether he have sufficient to finish it?

—LUKE 14:28–29

———

The Sled

February 2, 2014—the Big House, Tontitown, Arkansas

Technically, there was no problem with Derick and I being outside together that way. We weren't on a date or anything, so we didn't need a formal chaperone. Plus, there were easily a half dozen little Duggars running around out there with us, playing in the snow. We were safe. We were following all the courtship rules that my parents had encouraged us to write down—no holding hands, no in person, one-on-one conversations without another adult or mature chaperone present, no putting ourselves in a position where we could fall into temptation. All the same, I knew that people would be watching us. It was to be expected.

In between rides on the sled down the hill that runs away from the house, we were trading stories—Derick talking about the new job he was about to start, me telling him about my week as a student midwife. At some point the conversation was probably going to turn to the different wedding venues we'd been looking at. We were doing nothing unusual, nothing that any other couple of twentysomethings who are weeks away from getting engaged would hesitate to do. I was happy, at peace, and in love.

So I was surprised when I heard Mom call out, "Hey kids!" The snow was soaking up the sound, and it felt like the whole world was listening. When I turned to see her standing on the front porch, my stomach dropped. She was smiling that same smile the world has seen for years—a smile that's pure innocence but protects like a shield—and her voice was full of sweetness and joy. But I knew that voice well. By that point in my life I'd been obeying it for twenty-three years. I knew what was coming next.

"No boys and girls on the same sled!"

"Yes, ma'am," I said, jumping off the sled immediately.

But Derick didn't move. At least, he didn't back away from the sled—the scene of our crime. Instead, he was looking around. He was trying to figure out who my mom could have been addressing like that. Some of those little Duggars, maybe? A second passed. Then another. Finally, he stopped searching. His face shifted from curiosity to something like bewilderment. He turned back to the Big House, called out, "I'm sorry, Mrs. Duggar," and got to his feet.

I was grateful that he had gotten off on the other side of the sled from me, making sure it was between us—so that all the eyes that were currently upon us could see that we were not being disobedient.

"I'm sorry," I said quietly to him. "I should have known better."

Derick smiled. "It's no big deal, Jill. Really." But the bewilderment was still there. I could see it in his eyes.

One thing about growing up in the Duggar family, I saw a lot of bewilderment in a lot of different people's eyes. Cameramen, journalists, everyday strangers in a store. There was always someone staring, always someone trying to figure out if we were for real.

For years, I didn't pay it much attention. I either brushed it off or told myself that people's confusion about Duggar family life was just another sign that we had been blessed by God with a wonderful opportunity to show the world how we live. On that day in the snowy front yard with the empty sled between us and all those eyes on Derick and me, I was unable to see things clearly. It was the same a month later, when Derick proposed to me and I made sure that when I said yes, the film crew got the shot just how they wanted it. I couldn't see my life from the outside.

It didn't stay that way.

Soon, the bewilderment would be mine.

⊶⊷

CHAPTER ONE

Sweet Jilly Muffin

Click.

My parents didn't believe in magic. They didn't believe in dancing, either. But they understood the power of music. And like all magicians, they knew exactly when to wield it.

Just the sound of Mom loading a cassette into the tape player was enough to call us all to order. With one press of that button marked play, we would stop. We would listen. We would zip up our mouths, lock our feet on the ground and our eyes on Mom. We would be in her control completely, held by the three-second silence before the music would start, ready for whatever came next.

Sometimes it was a violin and a piano. Other times a rousing chorus of voices. On the rarest occasions we might hear drums, but only if they accompanied a marching band. It would take years before I would have the words to accurately describe and define the narrow genres of music we were allowed to listen to—a cappella hymns, southern gospel, certain classical pieces like Handel's Water Music. I was an adult by the time I could understand the reasons why these, and these alone, were the kinds of music that were allowed to fill the air of the Duggar household. But back then, in that sweaty living room, I didn't have any need for words. The music alone was enough.

I liked it best when Mom played "Ever in Joyful Song!" Almost immediately the violin was marching and spinning and twisting like a kite caught in a storm. All of us Duggar kids would get caught up in it, from my oldest brother, Josh, down to whichever baby would be old enough to rock on all fours, dribbling with delight.

At times, music was a distraction. Mom used it as a tool to break us out of a cranky mood or inject a little joy when it was needed. Other times she'd use it as a motivator to keep us on task as we folded laundry or unloaded groceries. Whatever the reason for pressing play, she used it wisely. Music had power, and it could be turned off as easily as it was turned on. Especially if someone mentioned the D word.

"Look," one of my younger siblings would say quietly to another little Duggar. "I'm dancing!"

Click.

Silence.

"Hey guys, listen," Mom would say, her sweetest smile back once more. "We don't dance. Remember, we want to be careful how we move our bodies, so we don't draw attention to the wrong areas. It's okay to jump for joy when we are excited, but we don't dance."

Most times the music would go back on, and we'd be allowed to continue. But if someone's joy jumping got a little too physical, it was either Handel's Water Music or game over: silence. Most of us Duggar kids knew the rules, but sometimes when friends were over, we had to stop because one of them was sticking their butt out, or—even worse—*shaking* it.

"We need to be very, very careful about the way that we move our bodies," Mom would say. "If you're shaking part of it, where do you think people will be drawn to look?"

We'd all chorus the answer together: "The part you're shaking."

"That's right. And you don't want people looking at your bottom, do you? You don't want people thinking bad thoughts about you, right?"

"No, ma'am."

"Remember what happened when King David was dancing in the street after returning with the Ark of the Covenant?"

"His wife despised him."

"That's right. He was dancing *and* he was immodestly dressed, and his wife despised him for it. Let's all remember that. When we are having fun, let's make sure that we don't move in a way that draws people's attention to places it shouldn't."

By the end of the talk, there was no more jumping.

Dancing was off-limits, so I learned from a young age how to be a hunter.

We lived in Springdale, Arkansas, a city of about 70,000 at the foothills of the Ozark Mountains, in a little house set on three quarters of an acre next to a church. There were cow pastures all around us, and being homeschooled like we were, we spent a lot of our

Jim Bob and Michelle, Josh, Jana, John-David, and Jill

days outside, drinking in that wholesome, northwestern Arkansas air. But I didn't hunt with a gun and I didn't lay traps. Instead of rabbit or quail, it was approval that I was searching for. And by the time I was old enough to balance a baby on my hip while I folded laundry—which I'm guessing was sometime around seven or eight years old—I was hands down the best approval hunter in the whole Duggar family.

When it came to getting a nod of acknowledgment or appreciation from Mom or Pops at the dinner table, or—best of all—being singled out for direct praise for listening intently while sitting perfectly quiet and perfectly still on one of the mauve-pink living room chairs during family Bible time at the end of the day, I tried my hardest to stand out as the most mature child in the room.

Whenever the tape player was turned on and we were jumping for joy, I always made sure that my movements were perfectly modest and that my jumping was perfectly straight. There was no wiggle whatsoever in my butt, no risk at all that the music would be turned off on my account.

"Stop, guys!" Pops might say when it was Bible time and Joy would be doing somersaults on the floor, and the twins—either set—would be wrestling for the best position on the couch. "You look like a can of worms! Look at Jill. She's got her notebook and Bible out and she's ready to go."

I wanted to be the good girl. I tried to be the perfect daughter. And my goal to be good and perfect even earned me a special pet name that only my parents used. I was *Sweet Jilly Muffin*, the fourth born, second daughter in the family. "Oh yeah," Pops would say whenever he was asked about his kids and he thought none of us were listening, "Jill's so sweet, so kind and caring. Out of all my daughters, she's the most like Michelle."

For an approval hunter like me, being compared to my mom like that was the greatest prize I could ever wish for. Mom was calm, self-sacrificing, and entirely loving. She seemed nearly incapable of anger or bitterness, and the love she had for her family only ever grew larger. With every new birth and additional sibling welcomed into the Duggar family, my respect and admiration for my mom only ever increased.

And Pops—my dad—Jim Bob Duggar? Well, that story's not too different either. From a young age I looked up to him. Just before our family reached double digits, he started bringing a few of us older kids with him to work at his car lot to give mom a break and

Jill and Jinger, mid-1990s

have some quality time with us older ones. He loved spending time with us and told us often that we were his number one hobby. I never tired of being around him, and it was a treat whenever we got to go with him to work. I'd watch him interact with customers— treating them well, being honest about the vehicles he was selling, and going the extra mile to help make things right on the rare occasion he ended up selling a lemon—and I knew that he was a good man. He was the same honest, upstanding, Christian man at work as he was whenever he was talking to us kids at home. He was the head of our household, and that was the way it was supposed to be.

So being Sweet Jilly Muffin was easy for me. The role of perfect daughter didn't feel like a role at all. It was who I was, who I wanted to be. In a family with as many kids as we had—twelve by the time I was nine years old—chaos was never too far away, and the opportunities to help out and be of service to the family were ever present. There was always a younger sibling who needed feeding, dressing or bathing, and when I'd helped all I could, I would play by filling an old medicine dropper bottle with watered-down Kool Aid, put it in my kid-sized apron with a few other items from my nurse playset, and do my rounds.

"Are you okay?" I'd ask each of my siblings in turn. "Do you feel sick at all? Let me give you a little something to help."

I was delighted when my parents introduced what became known as the buddy system. Each of us older kids would be given a younger sibling to help feed, dress and bathe, as well as to sit next to and buckle up when we went out anywhere in our fifteen-passenger van. I was the first one to sign up and get my own buddy, and I happily looked after my little sister Joy from when she was around one year old, and then my brother James when he came along. I was a ten-year-old girl whose parents trusted her with their precious babies. I felt like a little mom. I couldn't have been happier.

Mom was the most amazing teacher. Whether it was making flaky pie crusts for Pops' favorite pumpkin pies, or learning how to curl my hair just right, I relished any opportunity to learn from her. Spending time with Mom made me deeply happy, and an invitation to join her for a one-on-one outing to run errands—which often meant staying out way past bedtime—would leave me smiling inside for days.

Mom was a role model too. She always prioritized us kids and would wake up around the clock to care for us if we were sick. Even when she was sick herself she'd be awake all hours, dosing meds, handing out Popsicles, and bringing us wet rags to cool our fevers. In the highs as well as the lows, she taught me what it means to be a mother.

All I had to do to gain my parents' approval was to behave in a way Mom and Pops expected. And in the Duggar household, there were opportunities to remind us kids of those expectations and rules from sunup to sundown. Mom homeschooled us during the day, and Pops rounded off each evening by sitting in the living room or in the hallway between the girls' and boys' bedrooms and reading from the Bible as he talked to us about character and sin and everything else that mattered in life.

As a young child, I never experienced my parents as overbearing or domineering. Instead, in my young eyes, they were about as loving and fun and wonderful as any girl could hope for. At the end of each day they'd write us notes, affirming and encouraging us for whatever we'd done well that day—being kind to a sibling, working hard at our schoolwork, making the extra effort to help out. I never felt the need to push against their rules, and I never found either of my parents restrictive or constraining. If anything, I was grateful for the boundaries they laid down for our family. Even though I knew my parents were powerful and able to protect us, I was aware that there was a world beyond the land we lived on or the used car lot that Pops owned. And that world, as they reminded us over and over, was full of dangers and temptations and traps. Out there, my parents' protection could only go so far.

"Careful, girls! Let's be modest! Keep your dress down or tucked into your pantaloons."

Pops didn't have to remind us often, but sometimes when we'd be heading out on a bike ride, one of my younger sisters might need to be told. Whenever that happened, I'd check myself as a matter of course. Most of us would. We knew how important modesty was. None of us wanted to be accused of being "revealing."

As girls, Mom made almost all our clothes, and we only ever wore full-length skirts or dresses. All that dress fabric made cycling difficult, so Mom made us all full-length pantaloons to wear underneath. I appreciated my parents' careful eyes as they checked us for modesty. As I grew older, the fear that I might be immodest and cause someone to think bad thoughts would only get stronger.

It was even more difficult to stay modest the first time we went to a beach. We were visiting family in Savannah, Georgia, and took a trip to the beach one day. It was hot, and even though I was eight or nine, it was my first time seeing the ocean, my first time tasting salty air or feeling the sand between my toes. My first steps were cautious, like an astronaut on a new planet, but I loved it instantly.

But I was also troubled.

That trip to the beach was my first time seeing so many people wearing bathing suits in public. Even though my parents had been careful to take us to the quietest corner of the quietest beach, I could still see people in the distance wearing what looked to me like practically nothing—a few couples, lots of families. I didn't want to get any bad thoughts into my head, so I tried not to stare. But it was hard not to, and I worried for Pops and my brothers. Us girls had been told often how much harder it was for boys to keep their thoughts pure. I couldn't imagine the battles they were fighting out there on the sand.

Still, the beach was a new experience for all of us kids, and it brought out a different side of my parents as well. Soon they were caught up in the fun of the moment, cheering the little ones along as they ran and tumbled and played tag with the waves. We were all having fun playing in the shallow water, and like my parents, I got a little lost in the moment too.

The spell broke when I saw someone walking over toward us. It was a girl about my age, and she was heading right for us, riding the small waves on her boogie board.

"Why are you wearing those clothes to swim?" she said when she was close enough to get a good look at us. "Why are you not wearing bathing suits?"

"Uh, well," I said, caught between the fear of a lie and the awkwardness of talking to someone who was wearing little more than underwear in public. "We didn't plan on coming here so we didn't bring anything else with us."

The girl stared at me for a while. She took in my long dress with its now sandy hem and my blouse with its sleeves that reached almost to my elbows. I tried not to look at her golden skin. I kept my eyes on the waves instead.

I was grateful when the questions stopped and she ran back to the waves.

That day on the beach wasn't the first time I talked with someone who was so different from me, but it's one of the earlier memories that stands out the most. It was one of the first moments that I remember feeling awkward about the difference between the safety of my family and the strange lands beyond it. I tried not to dwell on it too much. I told myself that whenever we were in situations

2001

like that where we stood out, it was an opportunity to be a positive example to others just by living life and showing others how true, conservative Christians should live—set apart and unpolluted by the world.

We had a decent amount of friends, but those that we spent the most time with were all people my parents knew from our home church or were people with similar beliefs. On the rare occasions that I was given permission to visit one of their houses for a play date without my parents—though never on my own, always in the company of one or two of my siblings—I started noticing little things.

Some families listened to music that had drums in it.

Some allowed their girls to wear cycling shorts when it was hot and they were having a water fight outside.

Some homes had a TV.

And some kids even talked to me about having friends who went to public schools.

Instead of needing to keep any of this secret, I was grateful that my parents were happy for me to tell them whatever I had seen or heard when I was away from home. It was clear that they had thought carefully about how they wanted to raise us, and so they always had time for a discussion about the differences between our family and others—even though they took different approaches.

My parents liked to use role-play to prepare us for life.

"Okay," Mom would say at random, many times each week, usually during family Bible time in the evening. "What if somebody comes up to you and says, *Hey Joseph, why don't you read this book right here? It's got a witch in it.* What do you say?"

Joseph would deliver his line, right on cue: "I'm a Christian. I'm not able to do that."

"That's good Joseph. And what about you, Jinger? What would you say if someone asked you to watch a movie with them? The kind with people who are immodestly dressed."

"I would say. *I'm sorry. I'm a Christian. I'm not able to do that.*"

Mom's smile would turn up extra bright and we'd all get a clap. "That's right! And remember what we say to ourselves about the choices in front of us?"

This time it would be on all of us to reply, our voices singsonging in unison.

"Others may, we may not."

* * *

Mom's way of instructing us was true to who she is—a homemaker and full-time mama who knew how to nurture her babies with patience. Pops joined in the role-play games as well, but his approach was slightly different. He operated like a teacher or preacher, using illustrations to make his point, but mixed in a little politician and salesman who knows how to work a room. When it was his turn to mold us into the young men and women he envisioned, he was able to capture our imaginations by breaking down the challenges ahead of us into simple, binary choices.

"You've got the world over here," he would say during Bible time, holding his left arm far away from his body. "And then," thrusting his right hand far out in the other direction, "Christianity is over here. There's a line between them. Do you want to get as close to that line as you can? Do you want to walk so near to it that you might possibly be pulled into the world? Or do you want to steer as far away from it as you can get?"

"I want you to picture yourself on a table," he would explain. "It's much easier for somebody to pull you off the table than for you to pull them up. Now picture yourself with two or three people up there on the table with you. Maybe then it's a little harder for someone to pull you down, and a little easier for you to pull that person up on the table with you. That's how it is in life, and it's why you need to be careful who you spend your time with. Like my mom always told me, show me your friends and I'll show you your future."

His lessons made an impact on me. They worked on my siblings as well, because whenever Pops was talking with us like this—his voice a blend of warmth and warning—the whole room was silent.

There were lots of mini sermons and stories, but one always stood out more than most.

"I was about twelve or thirteen when I went to a seminar," Pops told us. "That was when I first heard about the power of music and the dangers of rock and roll. It's not just the lyrics but the music itself. When the drums get going, that backbeat has so much power over us. It can control us. That night, when I arrived home, I realized that the music I had been listening to was not Christ-honoring, because it was basically rock music with Christian words added on. I felt so convicted that I immediately got my eight tracks and took a hammer and busted them up."

I didn't know what an eight track was at first until Pops explained it, and I'd only ever heard rock music when we were out at a parade or a fair. Even my exposure to contemporary Christian music was limited at that time in my life. But I was captivated by the image of Pops being not much older than me, destroying his entire music collection because he wanted to follow God's lead in his life and live like a Christian should—set apart, with convictions. He had said that I was like my mom, but there were so many things about my dad that I wanted to emulate too.

The story became a kind of legend in our house, and we heard Pops repeat it often. We liked that it was both practical and inspirational and we could apply it to our own lives. We liked the idea of Dad taking a hammer to the devil like that, and we liked it because it marked the beginning of our family's involvement with a man named Bill Gothard, the man who had delivered the seminar that had made such an impact on Pops. Gothard was the founder and leader of IBLP (the Institute in Basic Life Principles), and eventually, when the film crews and excited whispers and stares from fans became a staple of our lives, the relationship between Pops and Gothard and his organization would become increasingly significant. And increasingly complicated.

But back in the days before we were on TV, things were simpler for us Duggars. We put into practice the lessons that Mom and Dad were teaching us, and we found our own ways of emulating our parents. For a while, all of us older kids and our friends formed different clubs, like the What Would Jesus Do Club, where a bunch of my sisters and a few friends would gather to make WWJD bracelets and talk about handing them out to people. There was another group formed in which us girls all read and discussed a book called *Beautiful Girlhood*. My sister Jana also formed a club that met in the shed and ate ice cream. I went to all of them regularly, especially Jana's.

These clubs were good, but the one I really wanted to join wouldn't let me in. And that bothered me.

One evening during Bible time, Pops told us that the local gas station had started selling pornography. We were all shocked and upset, and my older brothers Josh and John were determined to do something about it. They invited Steffan and Jeremiah, two of their fellow homeschool friends, and formed the Boys Christian Outreach Team—known as the Boycott Club for short. Their mission was clear: they planned to buy a load of Christian tracts—small leaflets explaining how to become a Christian—hand them out in town, and try to persuade everyone they knew to boycott the gas station. And if that wasn't enough, there was even a rumor that every time they met, they were going to eat pickles, *and* that Josh was going to cover them with his own homemade seasoning salt—a legendary recipe that Josh made himself with Lawry's seasoned salt, onion powder, lemon pepper, salt, pepper, and a few other secret ingredients.

The Boycott Club was where it was at, and I was desperate to join. But no matter how much I begged or how politely I asked, my application was refused on account of me being a girl. It was only when I offered two dollars to join that the boys agreed that the rules could be bent a little for me.

I was a little nervous before I attended my first meeting in the boys' bedroom. I was careful to sit perfectly still and silent as the four members sat in a circle, looking at the items Josh had placed on the floor in the middle: a locked money box, a small pile of tracks, a jar of dill pickles, and a container with his pickle salt inside.

"Okay," Josh said, calling the meeting to order. "So, first order of business is money. John, how much do we have?"

"Nineteen dollars and fifty-nine cents."

A warm murmur of approval went around the room.

"And Steffan, can you update us on the tracts?"

Steffan bent over the pile of Christian literature in front of him and pulled out a couple. "Some new ones came in the mail. I particularly like this one about not being left behind on the day of judgment."

Another warm murmur of approval.

"Good," said Josh. "My dad says that the gas station is still selling pornography, so we can keep encouraging people not to shop there."

And with that, it was pickle time.

*   *   *

Duggar kids, 1995

I never had to look far to be reminded of the ways that our family was different to others. It took an eleven-hour drive in our beat-up RV—that usually ended up lasting two days with the added stops and breakdowns—for me to discover how similar we were to others.

It was the mid-to-late 1990s. I was little at the time—too young even to have been given Joy as my buddy—but my memories are clear. We set out early in the morning and drove from our home in northwest Arkansas, taking Interstate 40 past Little Rock and all the way across Tennessee to Knoxville. It was a long drive, but the moment we arrived at our destination, we all knew it was worth it.

We were attending a conference in a basketball arena at the University of Tennessee, and the venue itself was enough to make my eyes pop. Bleachers rose high and wide, there were bright lights shining onto the stage, and a men's quartet was practicing while people rushed around onstage putting the blue curtains and green ferns in place. We found and occupied a row, way up high toward the back. Mom had given each of us a bag with a coloring book, a new box of crayons, and some snacks. Exciting as the bag was, I was too busy staring all around me.

Wherever I looked, there were people who were just like us. Families with identically dressed children—the girls in matching floral blouses and skirts that reached down to the ground, the boys in navy or khaki pants and button-down shirts. Parents marshalling their family units around the arena, some with four or five kids, others with closer to twenty. Having spent the first years of my life being taught how different we were from other people, it was almost shocking to see so many people who dressed like Duggars.

The conference was called Advanced Training Institute (ATI) family conference and had been organized by IBLP, the same group that was behind the seminar that had made such an impact on Pops. He and Mom had started to follow the teaching together soon after they'd gotten married, but this was our first trip as a family to the annual conference designed to encourage and equip homeschooling families like ours.

As the event got underway, I was spellbound by the music. The quartet sang in perfect harmony, and the whole auditorium was then led in a series of upbeat hymns—"We're Marching to Zion," "Leaning on the Everlasting Arms," and "Victory in Jesus"—all accompanied by a single, talented pianist.

The singing was powerful, but it was nothing compared to the moment when IBLP's founder and leader, Mr. Bill Gothard, took the stage. He was short and soft-spoken, but there wasn't a single person in the audience who wasn't listening to what he said.

Just like the clothes and the large families, what I heard was instantly familiar to me.

"Children are a blessing from the Lord!"

"Music can be a tool of the devil! Dancing is immoral and leads to sinful thoughts and behaviors!"

"If somebody was offering you a million dollars, would you refuse it? That's what you're doing if you're standing in the way of God's plan for you to have more children. Reject children and you are rejecting the very blessing of God!"

"Modesty is vital. Do not let yourself or your children lead someone into temptation."

Even though he spoke passionately about the value of children and the importance of large families, he was single. He had never married and had no children, yet I never heard anyone at any of the conferences take issue with it. Mr. Gothard wasn't like the rest of us. The usual rules didn't seem to apply to him.

He loved to quote scripture. The King James Version was the only translation used, so the language was old and dusty. But there was a power and authority in it, and I listened carefully, grateful for the clear rules that the Bible provided.

"Lo, children are an heritage of the LORD: and the fruit of the womb is his reward" (Psalms 127:3).

"The woman shall not wear that which pertaineth unto a man, neither shall a man put on a woman's garment: for all that do so are abomination unto the LORD thy God" (Deuteronomy 22:5).

"In like manner also, that women adorn themselves in modest apparel, with shamefacedness and sobriety; not with braided hair, or gold, or pearls, or costly array" (1 Timothy 2:9).

I was young, so I guess I only understood a fraction of everything I heard—and whenever Mr. Gothard started talking about "the seven basic principles of design, authority, responsibility, suffering, ownership, freedom, and success," I zoned out—but many of the words that echoed around the arena had been said many times by my parents at home. And looking around at the faces that were locked on the stage, I guessed that whatever Mr. Gothard was saying had to have been worth following.

Eventually Mr. Gothard stepped away from the lectern and invited other people up to join him. I watched as a handful of parents with young babies walked nervously onto the stage. "These are our reversal babies," said Mr. Gothard, at which point the whole arena exploded with applause. My siblings and I were confused, and Mom tried her best to explain over the noise of the clapping what a vasectomy was or how some women had their tubes tied, and the surgical procedures required to reverse it. A lot of the details went over my head, but the whole place was so full of joy that I didn't doubt for one minute that a reversal baby was a very good thing.

I didn't need any explanation when the next group of people were invited up. It was a family, a perfectly dressed dad leading a perfectly dressed mom, with eight perfectly dressed children following on behind. They all smiled as they moved with grace and elegance across the stage, arranging themselves in a perfect semicircle in front of a microphone. Mr. Gothard interviewed the dad briefly about how his business was prospering and how his family was such a blessing, then stepped back as the family prepared to launch into song.

The arena was silent.

Every one of the eight kids was smiling serenely as they sang.

The harmonies were nothing less than perfect.

This, I would later discover, was an IBLP tradition, and they were a Model Family.

Ahead of each conference, families could audition for the privilege of being invited onstage and perform a musical number in front of everyone. Some sang a cappella like this family, others brought their instruments and played along. The music was always impressive, but it was only a part of what made a Model Family special. They had to be modestly dressed, have a lot of kids, homeschool all of them, and play the right kind of music to the right kind of standard. But there was more to it than that. Model Families had to demonstrate the values that Mr. Gothard was preaching. Over the years I would learn from watching Model Families paraded onstage—as well as reading about them when they were profiled in IBLP newsletters—what it looked like when a family had devoted themselves to living a successful, God-blessed life.

Watching that family as they sang, and then listening to the applause once they had finished, it was clear that we Duggars were in some ways short of the perfection required to become a Model Family. When we played our instruments at home, the sound was sometimes painful to hear. We didn't keep a strict "early to bed, early to rise" schedule that we were told was essential to success. We could just about get everybody dressed the same, but it wouldn't ever take long before someone spilled, smudged, or dribbled mess on their clothes. We weren't Model Family material. Not yet, at least.

That IBLP conference in Knoxville marked the beginning of a new era in my life. Before it, my world had been small. We were like settlers in a new, hostile land. My life was almost entirely set at home—it was where we were schooled, where we played, and where we were taught how to live. Home was small, but it was a place of safety. It was our rock, and I knew every inch of it. The lands beyond it were vast and unknowable, beset with hidden dangers that lurked like quicksand.

But that trip east changed the way I saw things. We were not alone in the world. There were others just like us out there, people who looked like us, sang like us, and dressed like us. For the few days that we were there I had been able to let my guard down a little, and I was grateful for that. Mr. Gothard and IBLP had brought us together. He had brought us home.

I was delighted that our first trip to Knoxville was not our last. The annual conference became a regular fixture in our family calendar, and we also started attending other, smaller IBLP events throughout the year. Through these trips I learned more about what it meant to live according to Mr. Gothard's principles. At first my parents didn't send us out to any kids' groups, mainly because the groups cost money, but also because they preferred to keep us with them so we could get the full benefit of the teaching. I would sit and take copious notes on the importance of avoiding alcohol or submitting to the authority of my parents at all ages, even after marriage. Each seminar would end with a call for people to raise their hands as a sign that they were pledging to follow whatever IBLP principle had just been explained. I felt the pressure to prove my dedication to God, so it never took long before my hand was up in the air.

The more of the meetings I attended and the older I got, the more my worldview was shaped. I studied the people around me, especially the young women who were a few years older. Their dress was always modest, but some of them dressed professionally and wore perfectly tailored suit jackets with dress skirts, while others preferred more simple clothing—no patterns or bright prints, just muted, plain colors, no makeup, and maybe even a head covering. Most women I saw were smiling constantly, whether they were performing in the choir or orchestra, or just walking around. To my eyes, they didn't just look happy, they looked nearly perfect. Theirs was a wholesome, complete life.

I wasn't the only one paying attention or comparing myself to what I saw. One evening, not long after my first homeschool conference experience, one of the Model Families visited our area and a local church hosted a small event for homeschool families to hear them speak. The family played music and sang, then the parents spoke about their daily routine and gave tips on how they raised their children. At one point the mother explained a new concept she had started teaching her younger kids.

"We have always taught our children to address us with *yes, ma'am* or *yes, sir*," she said. "But we decided to take it a step further and teach them to say *yes, ma'am, I'd be happy to!* As Christian parents, it's our goal to raise godly, respectful, and obedient children. Our kids must learn to respect and obey their parents first, then eventually they will learn to respect and obey God."

I looked at my parents. They were both listening intently.

In the days that followed the event, my parents had us trying out the new concept at Bible time, role-playing *yes, ma'am/yes, sir, I'd be happy to!* In a short time, we had fully adopted the habit as our own.

IBLP wasn't the only expansion in our world at that time. My dad started to get involved in politics, successfully running for state legislature in 1998. Whenever it was in session, our whole family would move for four months to a rented house a little way outside Little Rock, Arkansas. Homeschooling would continue just as it always did, though sometimes instead of crowding around the kitchen table or learning outside in the far northwest of the state, some of

Duggar girls, June 1998

us older, more mature kids would be allowed to take all our study materials to the capital building while Pops worked. We'd tag along to the small committee meetings or occupy a corner of balcony area while Pops worked on the floor below. We weren't the only ones doing it, and there were even a couple of homeschool families whose dads were down on the floor while the children studied up on the balcony.

We picked up on some of the politics, but I mostly enjoyed chatting quietly with my friends, eating candy and other special treats some of Pops' co-workers would give us. My brother Josh, however, was fascinated. He'd get dressed up in a suit and tie and wander downstairs when the session was over. We'd watch him swagger beside Pops, a twelve-year-old politician in the making, shaking hands and talking about whatever bill had just been voted on. They called him the "Little Governor."

"Nike!"

That code word became just as powerful as the click of the tape player in a house full of Duggar toddlers. But while the press of the play button would send us into a blur of vertical motion, "Nike!" had the opposite effect. Whenever it was called out, everybody immediately looked at their feet. Nobody hesitated. Especially not the boys.

For as long as I can remember, my parents warned us regularly about the dangers of sin. They told us that sin came in many forms, like lying, stealing, disobeying our parents, or being a tattletale (which my parents called "stirring up contention among the brethren"). But perhaps the most dangerous and destructive sins of all were around sex and temptation.

At first, when we were much younger, the lessons were simple and clear-cut.

"Physical intimacy was created by God and reserved for marriage," they said frequently. "So the only person you should ever kiss is the one you marry, on your wedding day."

I liked this simple rule. It made sense to me.

But later, as we got older and the first of the Duggar kids approached puberty, the lessons became more complex.

It started one summer when I was around nine, Josh was twelve and the twins John-David and Jana were ten. It must have been around the time of either the Spice Girls or Britney Spears—neither of whom we had ever heard of—and whenever we went into town it seemed like every other girl we saw was wearing the kind of clothes that showed all their curves and most of their bellies.

At first we tried to ignore it, but with so many people following the fashion, it was almost impossible. Eventually, one day, when we were pulling out of a gas station, one of my older siblings cracked.

"Don't look!" they said as we passed by a particularly scantily dressed teenage girl. "There's a bad girl dressed immodestly over there!"

Mom turned around instantly and looked at us all in turn. She wasn't smiling.

"Children, be careful about how you speak of others and the words you use. You know, I do want you guys to protect your eyes, but I also want you to be careful not to think down about other people who dress a certain way. When you see someone dressed immodestly, it's okay to tell your siblings not to look, but don't put the other person down. That girl just doesn't know any better. It's not our place to judge. We should be praying for her instead."

She paused briefly. "When I was younger, before I was a Christian, I used to mow my lawn in a bikini. I really didn't know any better."

The silence that settled on us all was as heavy as a deep winter snow. To think that Mom was dressing so inappropriately at the same time Pops was destroying his music collection in pursuit of righteousness was kind of hard to comprehend. But Mom was the most godly woman I knew. Thinking about her transformation only made me love and respect her more.

Later that evening, at home during Bible time, Mom carried on the conversation. "You know what made me want to stop dressing like I used to? It was when I learned from your dad that men aren't like us girls. When women wear tight or revealing clothes that show certain parts of their skin between their collarbone and knees, it gets guys going and can stir up sensual desires. It can make them think bad thoughts. When girls do that to men, they're defrauding them. That's not good, and it can lead them to sin."

I think that was the first time I'd ever heard the word *defraud*, and it hung in my mind for a while. I didn't want to cause young men to think impure thoughts, and I purposed to never defraud, not by the way I dressed, not by the way I acted. I would be pure and live Christlike, even if it was difficult at times. Perhaps one day I would be worthy of a truly godly man.

Pops raised the issue with us as well, explaining that even though we all have bad thoughts at times, what mattered was how we dealt with them. "You have a choice about how you will deal with those thoughts. A thought becomes a sin when you dwell on it."

It was around that time that "Nike!" became part of the Duggar code. My parents were looking for a way to keep the boys from having impure thoughts, but wanted something more effective than simply telling them not to look whenever temptation walked by. "Nike!" was their solution. Whenever we were out and saw a female dressed badly—someone defrauding men by potentially planting bad thoughts in their minds—someone would call "Nike!" and everybody would immediately lock their eyes on their shoes until the all clear was given.

But Nike wasn't enough.

The dangers were not just out there on the street or in the mall, and they weren't just limited to the summer. They were closer to home, as I soon discovered.

I didn't know it at the time, but one problem was church. For as long as I could remember, we had attended Temple Baptist Church. The teaching wasn't quite the same as Mr. Gothard's, and I don't think there were any other IBLP families there, but it took a conservative line on most things, and people were kind to us even though we didn't share the same beliefs. My parents had always seemed happy enough with us going there, even if some of the other non-IBLP families had standards that were lower than ours—sending their kids to public or Christian schools and allowing them to hang out with the youth group and goof off when the service was over.

But it was at the end of the year when things went wrong. We attended a Christmas program at a different church and sat in silent horror as female members of the youth group—which no Duggar kid had ever been allowed to attend—performed a dance.

Later that night, Pops was somber as we settled down in our beds for Bible time.

"I am so sorry," he began, addressing us all but looking particularly at the boys. "You should not have had to have seen that. I was wrong to take us there tonight. We won't be going back to that church event again."

For a while, Bible time revolved around the theme of how hard it can be to do right even in Christian circles. Not every Christian held themselves to the same standard. "Sometimes," Pops said, "you have to be bold and learn to stand alone."

This must have gotten Mom and Pops thinking about Temple Baptist, because a short while later they announced that we had left and were going to be part of a new church that a pastor and homeschool father was starting. Pops let the church meet in a trailer house that he owned, and right from the start it reminded me of the ATI and IBLP conferences.

I don't remember what I felt about us leaving Temple Baptist. Some of that time in my life is blurred, the memories pulled out of focus. But I do remember the afternoon when Pops and Mom called me into their bedroom and closed the door. I was eleven at the time and they both looked pale and tired in ways I'd never seen them look before. I wondered if Mom had been crying.

"Hey," said Pops quietly. For once, the words weren't coming fast and freely. He had to search for them, to hunt them down. "Josh . . . has been talking to us. He has confessed about some stuff that he's done. Can we talk to you about it?"

I nodded. Sat quiet. And waited.

Waited for Pops to find the next words that he was going to say.

———⊸∞∞⊷———

CHAPTER TWO

"A Window of Opportunity that God has Given Us" (*and other half-truths*)

When Josh went away, we didn't talk much. The subject of whatever had happened with Josh wasn't embargoed and it wasn't off-limits, it's just that it wasn't something that I wanted to talk about so there wasn't much to say. Mom and Pops gave us the bare details about Josh, and so all I really knew was that he'd been sent away to stay with some of their friends, that he would be working construction, and that hopefully it wouldn't be long before he would return to us. That was all. I was happy to move on and put it all behind me.

As well as "Nike!", and all the other useful phrases that guided our steps, we had grown up being constantly reminded not to "stir up contention among the brethren." It was a way for our parents to keep us siblings from talking badly about each other, or putting anyone down, but over time it became something else—something more sinister. By preventing us from discussing anything contro-versial or sensitive with each other, the instruction not to "stir up contention among the brethren" became a tool for silence, for control, for guilt.

Despite being vague about Josh, my parents rarely missed an opportunity to involve us in other areas of life. Whenever there was work to be done around the house, from daily chores to maintenance and yard work, we would all be given a task, some tools and a clear set of instructions. Josh and John had both learned how to drive before they turned twelve, and by the time I was the same age I could teach my little sister to read, change diapers, babysit for short periods of time, and fix a meal for the entire family as well as any adult.

It was no different when it came to Pops' political ambitions. When he ran for state representative, we became his campaign staff. He mobilized the army of Duggars and drove us around northwest Arkansas, setting out lawn signs and handing out leaflets at events. We'd get Wendy's on the way home, and even when the days were long and the waiting was longer, it was good to be involved, especially when he won an initial term and then re-election. As kids, we had purpose. We weren't stuck in a classroom, exposed to all the perils of public school. We were out in the real world, helping Mom and Pops serve God within it.

That sense of purpose grew even greater the moment Pops told us that he had decided to run against the incumbent for the Republican nomination to the US Senate.

"Election to the United States Senate has never been something I have ever sought. It's not me that wants to run," he explained one day. "But I really feel like God wants me to do this. I've prayed about it and have done something that I only do for the most important decisions ever."

One of my siblings asked the question that we were all thinking. "What, Pops?"

"I flipped a coin three times," he said, his eyes growing wider, and a smile of amazement forming on his mouth. "And all three times it landed on heads. So I said, 'Okay, God, you want me to run, so I will run.'"

I was nearly eleven years old at the time and knew little of politics or the challenge of running against an incumbent, but I did know that senators and their families lived in Washington, DC. I didn't much like the idea of leaving Arkansas and the friends we had around us, but I also knew that sacrifice was an essential part of serving God.

"Ministry sometimes requires sacrifice," Mom and Pops would say often, before going on to quote Psalm 34:19: "Many are the afflictions of the righteous: but the Lord delivereth him out of them all."

So, we traveled the whole state, setting out yard signs, handing out leaflets and eating Wendy's on the way home. The days and distances covered were way longer than Pops' previous state campaigns, and the sacrifice felt real. And when primary polling day came around, and we all dressed in our matching outfits and accompanied Pops to the polling place—where a handful of journalists had gathered to tell the story—I was sure that a God-given victory was just around the corner.

I was wrong.

Pops lost.

His response was calm and measured. He reminded us that God had never told him he would win, just that he was supposed to run. He was satisfied that he had obeyed God's call, and I respected him for that. I also think us kids were a little relieved not to have to move to DC for several years.

But the loss was not the end of the story. In fact, it was really just the beginning of everything. One of those journalists who had interviewed Pops at the polling place was from the *New York Times*. He'd written about this crazy Christian guy with a bunch of kids, who had failed at the ballot box. The story had made it into print, alongside a photo of my parents and all fifteen of us Duggars lined up in a row, walking into the polling place, smiling cheerfully at the camera in our homemade, matching outfits.

A week or two later, Pops got a call from a magazine that wanted to know more about our family and run a feature about us. Pops wasn't sure at first, and he told them that our family was going through a difficult time, with their eldest son being temporarily gone and all. But he and Mom prayed about it, then told the rest of us that he wanted us all to pray and see if we felt that God was opening up a new opportunity for our family. We did what we'd been asked to do, and we all dutifully agreed that this was something God wanted us to do. Not that we had much choice in the matter.

After the feature came out—complete with a photo shoot with all of us (minus Josh) out in a field somewhere, surrounded by hay bales—Pops played a message on our answering machine from a man who said he was from Discovery Health and that he wanted to make a one-time documentary about our family. Pops was skeptical.

"I don't want you to make us out to be freaks," he said when he called the guy back.

I didn't hear the other end of the conversation, but as I listened, and for a long time after the conversation, Pops looked serious. He looked like he did whenever he was listening hard to Mr. Gothard or one of the other lawmakers in the state house of representatives.

"You know," said Pops to all of us later at Bible time, "when I ran for senate, I didn't see God's ultimate purpose in it. But with the article and now this TV documentary, I'm beginning to see that God had something bigger and better in store for us. This is a window of opportunity that God has given us to show people what a Christian family can look like. This is our chance to share with the world that children really are a blessing from the Lord."

I didn't know it at the time, none of us did, but that phrase—"a window of opportunity"—would become as familiar in the Duggar house as the cries of a newborn baby, or the call of a director for there to be quiet on set. Mom and Pops would repeat those five words often, and just like the call of "Nike!", "a window of opportunity" became part of our family shorthand. It was an instant explanation of the reasons why certain choices were made, a reminder of the blessings received and the sacrifices that all of us must make in return. But with every passing season and every change that would follow, the meaning of those five words would alter. In time, whenever I would hear anyone talk about how that first decision to bring the TV cameras into our home was a window of opportunity, all I would think about was secrets and lies.

I was grating cheese when the film crew showed up.

"Just act normal," I was told by a man with an earring, as a camera loomed in front of my face and a woman wearing pants started instructing everyone in my family what to do. I was twelve now, a mess of self-conscious nerves and red-faced awkwardness. Acting normal was not an option. I tried to relax, digging out my best Sweet Jilly Muffin smile for the viewers.

"Look over there, sweetie. Don't look at the camera!"

It wasn't easy acting natural, especially when they had us all line up in our pj's outside the bathroom door. They wanted to show the viewers that we all shared the two bathrooms in the house, but it left me feeling embarrassed, uncomfortable, and a little unsafe. Not that I could express any of that to my parents. This was a God-given window of opportunity, after all. The best thing I could do was bury my feelings.

It wasn't all bad. At one point the woman wearing pants announced that the TV crew was going to follow us to the store for groceries. As we pushed our five shopping carts around Aldi, I heard a whisper that the crew was going to be paying for everything. So, for the first time ever, Mom wasn't directing us to buy our usual stocks of canned beans, ramen noodles, and forty-eight-cent frozen beef and bean burritos. Instead, we were allowed to fill our carts with boxes of Lucky Charms and Honeycomb cereals, ice cream sandwiches, frozen pizzas, and all-beef chimichangas. Our carts were heavier than ever before, and all of us Duggar kids had the same double-wide smile fixed on our faces. For once, the week ahead wasn't going to be filled with tater tot casserole or bean sandwiches.

The TV crew visited us for two or three days that first time, then returned for another few days every two or three months. It was a long, slow process, and it got so that we hardly noticed them when they were with us, and missed them when they left and our weekly menu returned to its usual staples of beans, tuna, and macaroni.

By the time *14 Children and Pregnant Again!* was complete, Josh had returned to live with us. His head had been shaved, I guess in an attempt to punish him or instill some humility. I wasn't worried about him, though. I was a kid, and I trusted that things would get better now that Josh had been "fixed." Besides, it felt right to be complete as a family again, especially as Mom had given birth to Jackson, the fifteenth Duggar child. Pregnancy wasn't easy for Mom, especially in the first trimester when the nausea was bad, but we loved the excitement that surrounded a new baby. To have another sibling to love on and care for made me deeply happy.

For a while, the baby eclipsed the filming. We had been sent a DVD to approve the forty-five-minute documentary, but still didn't have TV in the house, so by the time the show aired, I'd started to forget about it a little.

That didn't last long.

14 Children and Pregnant Again! went on to become the number one show on Discovery Health at the time. Pops was ecstatic.

"We prayed about it as a family," said Pops at Bible time one night, his eyes dancing with excitement. "We felt like God was wanting us to share with the world the message that children are a blessing from the Lord, and now it's the number one show on the channel! God is blessing this! God is using us to share his message with the world!"

From that moment on, we didn't just talk about a window of opportunity. Now we had a new name for what we were doing: it was our "ministry."

*   *   *

Duggar family at old Johnson Road house, 1993

The Duggar family kept on growing, and by the time Mom gave birth to Johannah, her sixteenth, the TV crews were regular visitors to our little home surrounded by the cow pastures. It was getting crowded in there, with only two bathrooms and three bedrooms, so Pops bought some land over near Tontitown and started the long process of building us a brand-new, seven-thousand-square-foot steel-framed home. I was too young to even begin to wonder where the money came from and was just happy at the prospect of a little more space at home. We moved into a rental while the new house was being built, and in true Duggar style, we did as much of the work as we could—laying the radiant heat flooring, tiling the floors and a whole lot more besides. But even though we were able to dedicate plenty of time to the project, and our workforce was big, the house was bigger. A build which we hoped would be ready in a year was still in progress when Mom announced that she was pregnant with her seventeenth baby.

The arrival of another Duggar meant we had ourselves a deadline, but our growing number wasn't the only reason to hurry up our work. A second documentary had shown us starting the work on the house, but the producers wanted the third Duggar TV special to feature us actually completing the work and finally moving in. Thanks to some good negotiating from Pops, the network agreed to get out the checkbook.

Duggar family in front of the Big House while still under construction, 2004

If we'd been excited about filling our shopping carts with free Honeycomb cereal, frozen pizzas and chimichangas, this was a whole other level. A crew of workers turned up to the site, and the producers flew in an interior designer from New York. She helped us pick out the kind of bedroom sets and other furniture that we would never have been able to afford. There was still a ton of work for us to do, but seeing the Big House (as we always called it) sprinting toward the finish line like that made all the long hours worthwhile.

I don't know when I first heard Pops describe us as "a filming family," but it made sense to me. We studied as a family, we worked as a family, we did everything as a family. Neither Mom nor Pops had hobbies outside of us, and I was thankful for that. They were devoted to each other and devoted to us. We were an everything family, so why not let the cameras come in and show the world?

There was a fourth documentary—which followed us on a road trip—and then a fifth, which covered the birth of Jennifer, the seventeenth Duggar kid. As a "filming family," we were opening our home and letting the world come on in and take a look. By this point I was sixteen and no longer blushing every time the camera came near me. The crew was almost becoming part of the family, and I was willing to take whatever direction I was given. This was our window of opportunity. This was our ministry.

So when Mom and Pops told us that the network, TLC, wanted to move on from one-off documentaries and start making an actual reality show about us, I wasn't blown away with surprise. It was just another confirmation of the fact that this whole thing was a God-ordained opportunity. To my mind, at least, it had nothing to do with us wanting to be famous or see ourselves on TV. After all, we still didn't even have a TV in the house and we would only watch the rough cuts of each documentary when they were sent over on DVD. I was vaguely aware of when the shows were being broadcast, and strangers might say something nice to us from time to time about what they'd seen of us on TV. But when Pops asked us to pray about whether we should say yes to TLC's offer, the prospect of becoming famous was the last thing on my mind, especially when Pops explained the condition that he'd made with the network.

"I told them that our faith is the core of our lives, so they cannot edit out our faith. They said it's our story, and that we can tell it however we want."

In the world of IBLP, it was never okay to say you were proud of anything or anyone, no matter how godly the person or righteous the decision. But even though I knew Proverbs 11:2 and 16:18 by heart ("*When* pride cometh, then cometh shame," and "Pride *goeth* before destruction, and a haughty spirit before a fall"), I was kind of proud of Pops for telling TLC that our faith was nonnegotiable. I believed in what we were doing and prayed that God would give my parents the guidance they needed as they negotiated.

"They're calling it '17 Kids and Counting,'" he announced one day, letting the words hang in the air a little as we heard the title for the first time. "This is a ministry opportunity that God has brought to us. If it were over tomorrow, we would be happy."

I looked around at my siblings. Nobody disagreed. It seemed to me as though we were of one mind, united. We trusted Mom and Pops completely. Whatever happened with the show, however long it lasted, I was convinced that it could only ever be a good thing.

I was sixteen when the individual documentaries turned into a reality show series, and I was old enough to notice the different demands that it placed on our family. The first five documentaries had been filmed over a period of almost three years, but we shot the whole of the first season of *17 Kids and Counting*—all ten episodes—in a few months. The crew would come three days each week, filming three hours in the morning then another couple in the afternoon or evening, sometimes a little more, sometimes a little less, depending on the week. Once all the Duggar family content had been shot, we'd have a series of interview days in a local studio where we'd narrate the show. It ran like this for weeks on end, and homeschooling was often interrupted so that we could get out of the house and film something fresh and new for the show—like taking a trip to New York City for sightseeing or driving up to Ohio for a family reunion. These experiences were exciting, opening the world to us. Nobody complained, and I guess we just accepted it when Bible times didn't only include praying and reading the Bible together, but also became more extensive briefing times, with Pops and Mom reminding us of upcoming filming commitments, as well as cautioning us to not tell other people about what we were doing. We were a filming family now, so we had to take it seriously.

Aside from the filming trips, the new show marked the return of the old perks we'd enjoyed when *14 Children and Pregnant Again!* was shot. If we went to Aldi in the weeks we were filming, our carts would be filled without us worrying about the price. On days that the crew was with us they would order in food from wherever we wanted. Pops even gave us older kids a debit card, so that if we were out running errands or hauling the younger ones to a music lesson or dental appointment and it was getting late in the day, we could grab food out on the way home and give him the receipts. It was a whole lot better than how it used to be, with us driving around with a Crock-Pot of chili, feeding the little ones on the run.

We were already deep into filming the second season when the first one aired. Just like with the documentaries, we didn't always watch them live but had carefully checked over the various rough cuts that had been sent over to us. Just like Pops had told them, they hadn't edited out references to our faith, and when the show aired, I was excited at the thought of all those people across America watching and getting to see Christian values lived out on a secular television channel and maybe inspiring them to live for Christ.

It wasn't just random strangers who were watching us and taking note of how we lived. One day we were told that we were soon going to host a special visitor for lunch. A delegation of IBLP leaders from Romania was visiting the US, traveling with several of the main leaders, including Mr. Gothard himself. They were going to be in the neighborhood, and they were going to visit us for lunch.

The excitement was instant. But then came the challenge. The Romanian delegation totaled about fifty people, and there were almost as many US IBLP leaders accompanying them. The Big House had two kitchens, one regular-sized and the other a full commercial one with an industrial dishwasher and super-wide ovens, so we had the capacity to cook for large numbers, but not the pans required to prepare lunch for almost one hundred people. Mom put out a call to her friends from church, and a small army of wives and some of their kids descended to help clean, cook, and prepare for this epic event.

There was no filming that day, but even if the crew had been there, I doubt we would have noticed them. When we heard the buses turn off the road and roll down our gravel drive, we all took up our places out front. We'd rehearsed our family greeting a couple of times, and lined up in age order, ready to extend a hand, as we put on our brightest IBLP smiles and introduced ourselves.

We'd sometimes practiced this at Bible time over the years, especially for the newest younger kids to learn the drill, and it had always gone well. With the Romanians, however, we hit a little turbulence. Both the men and women among them didn't just want to shake our hands, they greeted every single one of us with a kiss on each side of our face. Aside from the occasional handshakes and side hugs at church, or when being examined by the dentist or the occasional visit to the doctor when we were sick, kids in the Duggar family weren't supposed to have much physical contact with the opposite gender. But even though the greeting line lasted forever and was awkward—all of us older kids were blushing—we accepted it as a cultural difference. Besides, the presence of Mr. Gothard was enough to push any embarrassment to the background.

I wasn't surprised by how short he was, as I'd seen him up close before, but I'd never seen him outside of a conference, especially not in Arkansas in our home. Having Mr. Gothard visit us at the Big House was a huge deal. In my opinion, having such a man of God visit our home was more impressive than being greeted by a fan in an airport, and even more impressive than a visit by the president himself. Mr. Gothard was different from a boisterous politician, but also very similar with his charm. At a little over seventy years old, with black dyed hair, a round face and a wide smile, he had a twinkle in his eye as he looked straight at each person he addressed. His voice was soft, with a strong northern accent, and he gave each of us a firm handshake as he slowly moved down the line. Watching him come closer, greeting my parents first, then my youngest siblings, I could feel the nerves mounting within me.

When it was finally my turn, I thrust my hand out and blurted out the words I had been rehearsing for days.

"If it weren't for you, Mr. Gothard, I likely wouldn't be here!"

He looked intrigued. His smile growing even wider. I stammered on.

"My parents have always told me that they would have stopped having children after they had the twins, numbers two and three. I'm number four, so thank you for teaching them that children really are a blessing from the Lord!"

I don't remember what he said in reply, but I know what I felt, and it wasn't embarrassment or awkwardness. In my eyes and the eyes of everyone I knew, Mr. Gothard was a legend, a man who we all looked up to. To have his attention on me for just a few seconds was enough to leave me feeling on top of the world. As Sweet Jilly Muffin, approval hunter, it was a moment that I would treasure for the rest of my life.

* * *

The Duggar favorite lunch of tater tot casserole and sauteed green beans (from a cookbook written by the Voellers, one of the best-known Model Families) must have been a success, because from then on, we found ourselves invited to a whole bunch of IBLP events. Sometimes my parents would be invited to speak, and occasionally we got free lodging and entry into the kids' activities that we previously hadn't been able to afford. We were starting to become a Model Family. Along with some of my sisters, I was invited to attend one of their camps called Journey to the Heart up in Michigan. We were invited to serve as leaders, which was a great honor that I hadn't expected at all. Even more surprising, though, was the fact that after the camp, my elder sister Jana was personally invited by Mr. Gothard to visit IBLP headquarters in Chicago and work there for a while. We were new to the inner workings of IBLP, but we knew enough already to understand why it was only Jana who was invited. She was the only elder Duggar girl who was blond, and everybody knew that Mr. Gothard liked blond girls. We'd joke about it, calling Jana one of "Gothard's Girls." It didn't occur to me at all how strange, unsafe, and unwise it was. And if I had, I doubt I would have been able to speak out against it. Sweet Jilly Muffin had grown up, but I was still terrified of conflict and would do anything I could to avoid it.

I was sixteen the day some of the families from church had come over to the Big House. It was one of those hot summer afternoons when it was impossible to stop sweating, especially when we were all wearing full-length skirts. I'd outgrown wearing the pantaloons a few years earlier when I'd stopped climbing trees and learned to keep my skirt down at all times, but I felt bad that some of the little kids were getting kind of cranky in the heat. So I got permission from my parents to set up a water balloon fight.

It was fun, and everyone was having a good time, shrieking and yelling out as we chased each other across the grass. But then a voice I didn't recognize yelled out.

"Stop! What are you doing!?"

I froze, a large tub of water balloons heavy in my hands. I turned to see one of the dads, red-faced with more than just the heat. He was enraged that his kids would be playing like this without his permission, and the veins were popping above the buttoned-up collar of his shirt. He was yelling at the top of his voice, gesturing for his thirteen kids to immediately run toward him. They all obeyed instantly.

"Who gave you permission to do this? Answer me! Who allowed this?"

Nobody answered, and he kept on yelling. In the chaos I slipped away, ran to the end of the house that was farthest away, and locked myself in the bathroom. It must have taken me ten or twenty minutes for my heart rate to get back to normal, and another hour at least before I was brave enough to unlock the door. I guess I inherited my avoidance of conflict from Mom. I doubt it was from Pops. When the show was just beginning and we were acclimating ourselves to our new life as a filming family, something wholly unexpected happened. Something that made Pops upset in ways I'd never seen before.

It started with a letter.

Way back before Josh had been sent away, around the time we had left the church that had allowed immodest dancing at its Christmas service, Josh had been courting a girl. He must have confessed to her vaguely about the abuse that he had committed, because I heard later that the girl had written a letter to him, expressing her anger at what he'd done. But instead of sending it to him, she'd tucked it away in a book.

Four years later, in 2006, the book was loaned to a friend at church and the letter resurfaced. It was read by someone who knew us, someone who attended the same church as us. Instead of talking with Mom or Pops, she got more information from church leadership, phoned a hotline, and informed DHS about what she thought was a potentially abusive situation.

Everything changed when we were in Chicago to record with Oprah and then attend our first IBLP Headquarters Christmas party. Pops received a call notifying him of the investigation, and as soon as the trip was over, myself, most of my sisters, and my parents all had to be interviewed. We attended a closed-court session. People—strangers—would come to our house at random times to make sure there were locks on the doors and that everybody was sleeping where they were supposed to be sleeping.

It was terrifying.

I was frightened that I was going to say the wrong thing and that someone was going to take us away from Mom and Pops. *One wrong word, one bad answer, and I'll be the one who tears our family apart.*

I tried not to let my fear show, I tried to bury it deep inside. But I was older now and there was more at stake—it didn't just affect me, it affected all of us. So it was harder to bury the fear caused by the investigation than the fear caused by the abuse that DHS was looking into.

Mom and Pops took time to sit with us all, to pray with us and explain as best they could what was going on. I appreciated it, especially their advice.

"Just tell the truth," they both said, many times. "It's a safe place and they're just doing their job. Tell the truth and everything will work out fine."

I was bound up tight in my own fear, but not so tight that I didn't notice the way that Pops was feeling too.

He was angry.

I had heard that the person who had found the letter and phoned the hotline had also talked to a few other people in our church. While the details remained private, the story of my brother having problems spread throughout our small home church. Some families treated us kindly and with compassion, but I believed others were jealous of our success with the television show and treated us with suspicion. "They threw us to the wolves," Pops said when the investigation concluded. "They did not stick up for us at all. They're the ones who made this happen. They're the ones who allowed DHS to investigate our family, even though we had already taken care of it."

The fallout was immense. We didn't know who we could trust, who was for us or who was against us. We pulled back from the church, no longer allowing them to host services at the Big House. It created a deep divide within our church, and in time, inevitably, I guess, the church split.

Like Pops, I was hurt and angry.

But when it was over, all I wanted to do was put it behind me. I had been terrified of losing my family and traumatized by the questions I had been forced to answer. I wanted to forget all about it. I wanted to move on from the whole thing—as fast and as far away as possible.

CHAPTER THREE

Clipped Wings and Hills to Die On

I sat up straight, checked my skirt once more, and prepared my brightest smile. A quick glance left and right told me that Jana, Jessa, and Jinger were all doing likewise. It was one of our first public appearances since the release of our book in March 2014 about our lives and our faith, called *Growing Up Duggar*. I'd been kind of unsure about it at first, but it had been way easier than I thought. Pops had taken care of everything, from the writer who helped us with the words to dealing with the publisher. He'd even told us that since there was an advance, he had been able to buy us some new, gently used harps.

Writing was unfamiliar, but talking was easy. So at this impromptu Q&A at a bookstore in North Carolina, we all knew what was expected of us. We knew the unwritten script that we needed to follow.

"How do you kids feel about the show? Do you like it?"

"Oh, it's a family ministry," said Jana. "You know, sometimes it's hard, but the film crew is like family to us."

"We love having them in our home," I added, wanting to wipe away any hint of a negative from my sister's answer.

"And how long do you think it's gonna go?"

"Well, I don't know about that," said Jessa, "but I do know that we just feel like it's a window of opportunity that God has given our family."

"And we'd be happy if it was over tomorrow," said Jinger. "We're just leaving it up to God."

It was all true, but it was not the whole truth. Even in the early days, my feelings were not quite as simple as the script we were

The crew filming in the girls' room at the Big House

following. Season one had been a hit. So were seasons two and three, which followed soon after, airing a total of forty-eight episodes throughout 2009. All that success meant that the rhythm of our lives was increasingly set by the filming that was now taking place for ten or eleven months of the year.

The perks were still good. We got to travel more—Mom and Pops went to San Francisco for their twenty-fifth wedding anniversary, and a bunch of us flew down to El Salvador for a mission trip. but some of the best times were the simplest ones, like a road trip to DC or to Branson, Missouri, and Silver Dollar City. We'd crowd into our old RV with the back window open and make a game of getting the semi drivers to honk at us. We'd park in a Walmart parking lot to sleep at night, then stock up on Little Debbie oatmeal cream pies, deli chicken tenders, and potato wedge fries as soon as the store opened the next morning.

I loved these times when we were all together, especially when it was just us Duggars. The presence of the film crew brought plenty of good things, but I quickly grew to dislike the way they sometimes wanted to spring surprises on us. I guess it made for good TV to see us react in real time to the news of whatever challenge or adventure they'd set up for us, even if it was just an escape room or a trip to a park, but it got to the point where I was feeling the stress nearly every time they were filming. Either I was trying to bury my discomfort and anxiety when they sprung a surprise on us, or fake my joy when we were filming something we'd already rehearsed. I had to keep my reality far away from the TV.

With the increasing success of the show, we also started attracting some negative attention. We had a family blog that people would use to contact us, and at first Pops did all the sifting through emails, having warned us against reading anything that came through it. He also warned us about any negativity we might see online or hear about in other places, reminding us that "People are going to say negative stuff. There will always be naysayers."

There wasn't much access to the internet for us in those days, and there was a soft rule that we couldn't do social media until we were married. But while Pops could handle most of the emails, the amount of physical mail that people sent to our home was starting to pile up. Some of us girls began to help sort through it all and respond to people when possible. Most of the time the mail was overwhelmingly positive and kind, but from time to time we'd receive something negative. It might be a letter with packets of condoms inside, an all-caps message telling us to STOP HAVING KIDS YOU'RE OVERPOPULATING THE EARTH, or just plain old hate mail telling us we were horrible people. Our parents would always respond with the same advice: "When you're doing what's right, you're always going to be persecuted. Don't ever forget that Jesus was persecuted, and he never sinned once in his whole life."

I took comfort from their words. Despite the fact that I was hardwired to search for approval like a sunflower that scans the sky, these negative reactions didn't bother me too much. Instead of feeling crushed by them, I actually felt encouraged. All my life I'd been taught that ministry comes with hardships, that following God inevitably involves suffering. So in some ways, this negative feedback was a kind of relief. Having been to El Salvador and seen the conditions that the Indigenous Christians were experiencing down there—no electricity, no running water, a constant humid heat and no AC—and frequently hearing from missionaries in other places who lived in similar conditions and some even worse, I was already starting to feel that the ministry that God had called us Duggars to was way less challenging than others. Seeing the hate mail as a light form of persecution for the sake of Christ somehow slightly eased my guilt. It made me feel a little better about things.

I feel like the success of the show also changed the way that we were viewed by the leaders of IBLP. We were still way less polished than the other Model Families, but the fact that we were airing almost every week of the year made us appealing in other ways. Instead of educating and resourcing the existing followers of Mr. Gothard, we were introducing millions of new people to the world of IBLP. It didn't go unnoticed, and as well as us girls being invited to help out at camps, or volunteer at the main offices, the leaders started asking Pops for his input on decisions as well.

Pops was happy to oblige. He would tell us kids all about how he'd talked with Mr. Gothard on this matter or that, how he'd recommended a certain person speak at a conference. He seemed to enjoy this new position, but he wasn't only talking to Mr. Gothard or the other leaders. Pops often offered encouragement to parents. Many times I'd heard him talking with couples about their children, offering them advice like "You need to train them to understand why they believe what they believe," or "The Bible says to 'train up a child in the way he should go: and when he is old he will not depart from it.' We as parents are responsible to God for how we raise our kids." Pops was never shy about telling the truth, even when it hurt a little.

Pops was aligned with the way IBLP saw the world. Those "seven basic principles" that were the core of everything made sense to him and had shaped the way he and Mom brought us up. Mr. Gothard's teaching determined what little music we could listen to, the cut of our clothing, and the length of our hair. We would be home-schooled and hardly ever allowed to spend time in the company of anyone who wasn't either our parent, an older sibling, or—on rare occasions—a friend from church. There would never be any drink-ing, any dancing, or even any contraception once we were married.

"Children are a blessing from God" was a fundamental state-ment that underpinned so much of what IBLP taught, but so was the subject of authority, especially the authority of parents over their children. A portion of scripture that was frequently taught or refer-enced was "Honor thy father and mother; (which is the first com-mandment with promise;) that it may be well with thee, and thou mayest live long on the earth" (Ephesians 6:2–3). Honoring par-ents—even into adulthood—was such a big deal that even if your parents weren't Christian, it would be a sin to disobey them. If you wanted to get married and they refused to give their blessing, IBLP teaching was on the side of the parents.

There wasn't a lot of talk about hell or damnation, but fear was a powerful tool within IBLP. TV, public school, even contempo-rary Christian radio stations with their rock music—these were all threats constantly trying to drag us away from righteous Christian living. Children needed to be protected from them all, and so there was a lot of talk about "umbrellas of protection"—one of the most significant planks of IBLP teaching. If a child ever were to disobey their parents' instruction, or act in a way that dishonored them, they would be placing themselves at risk. By disobeying their parents, they would be stepping out from under the umbrella of protection, and terrible things could happen. By turning themselves over to sin, God's judgment would be on them.

In the world of IBLP, the parents' authority didn't end when their child turned eighteen or even on the day they were married. They still talked about the Bible's teaching of "leave and cleave," and how couples should make decisions together, but it seemed like they didn't really believe it when it conflicted with the parental authority teaching. It might change or look different, but parental authority never stopped, never weakened. Like all my siblings, I knew that I would always strive to honor and obey my parents, even when I was married and had kids of my own. Saying no, going against Mom's or Pops' wishes, it wasn't something I could ever imagine myself doing, especially since our beliefs aligned in most areas. Many times my parents had told us that one day we'd get married and do things a little differently than they had. "That's okay," they'd said, and so I believed that when the time came, if my husband and I made some different decisions about things from the way I was raised, those decisions would be respected.

However, even though I couldn't see it at the time, IBLP also encouraged parents to clip their children's wings. They taught that children should stay with their parents until marriage, and that instead of going away to college, children should stay home and pick up other safer trades for work. They encouraged fathers to be self-employed, to build up family businesses and have their boys

work for them. It was a clear way of keeping full-grown, adult off-
spring locked into the role of dependent children. Back then, seen
through the eyes of my younger self, it seemed like a great plan. I
didn't have any intention of leaving home or trying to make a life for
myself on my own. Why would I? The world was dangerous and full
of peril. At home, in the Big House where my parents could protect
me, things were safe.

But no matter how much Pops tried to keep our wings clipped or
how badly he tried to keep us huddled in close underneath his own
personal umbrella of protection, there was one child he couldn't
prevent from making mistakes. It was Josh. A few years after he was
first sent away, he was in trouble again. He'd been caught looking
at pornography on the phone of somebody he'd been working with.
Those seven basic principles didn't have much to say about secular
therapy or rehab, so once more, Josh packed his bags, and Pops sent
him away from home for several months to do some demanding
manual labor in the company of good Christian folk and get himself
back on track.

And just like before, we didn't talk about it much.

Josh's problems were only ever talked about vaguely, if at all,
but Pops was happy to answer most all questions we had about the
show (unless those questions were about money). He would explain
the daily responsibilities, the upcoming events, and often encourage
us by sharing positive feedback he'd had from people. It left me in
no doubt that the show was being used by God to minister to the
nations. Pops would say yes to almost any positive filming opportunity that came along, and we even ended up with crews from all
over the world coming to Tontitown to film with us for their own

specials. I remember one time when a crew from South Korea came. They were very kind but set a much more punishing schedule than we were accustomed to, filming five days in a row from seven in the morning until ten and sometimes even eleven at night. I don't remember so much about the Russians other than that they were more laid-back and spent time explaining to us how their previous plan to fix their declining birth rate was to give people refrigerators in return for having babies.

With every season of the show that went out on TLC, and every one-off program that Pops signed us up for, I could see him grow. He had sold his old used-car lot and vehicle towing service back when he'd entered politics but had kept his car dealer's license up-to-date and still loved going to car auctions. He rented some land to Josh that he used as a car lot, and sometimes Pops would put some of his own vehicles out on Josh's lot to sell. As the show grew, Pops got more into buying real estate and focusing on maintaining what he had, but whenever he was talking about the show and the ministry impact he thought it was having, he really came alive.

"I've always had this great desire to reach people for Christ," he said one day not long after he'd returned from a trip to New York City, where he and Mom, Jessa, Jinger, and Jordyn—the newborn eighteenth Duggar—had appeared on *The View*. "When we were flying in over the city, I was asking myself, how could we reach this many people for the Lord? And then it occurred to me that there are so many people watching the show. We're reaching millions. I never would have dreamed that God would allow our family to have this influence over all these people."

I shared his amazement that we had ended up in this position. It was wild and crazy that a family like ours from northwest Arkansas should end up like this just five years after the first documentary, and it was even more wild and crazy that we'd done nothing at all to make it happen in the first place. The only possible explanation was that God had opened the doors for us. He had made a way. This show, being a filming family, this was his calling on our lives. For now, at least.

The NYC story became one of Pops' favorites. I heard him tell it often, especially when it seemed like he wanted to help someone understand that we really weren't in it for the perks or the fame or anything like, or he needed to explain that the show came to us and that we didn't go looking for it. Ever the salesman, Pops always seemed to know how to pitch it right, and his story always worked. At least, it appeared to work until the one time that it didn't.

I heard about it weeks later. A young man who was a family friend had apparently been talking with Pops one day at the Big House. Pops had been trying to persuade the guy to agree to be in some filming, talking about the ways he believed that God was using the show to impact so many people, inferring that the numbers reached by our show on television had a greater impact than lots of other ministries.

"Think about how many people we are able to reach through the show!" Pops had continued. "Oftentimes we are reaching people who would often never step foot into a church, yet they invite us into their living rooms each week! It's such a huge opportunity God put right in our laps, and we should be good stewards of what he has given us!"

"That's very interesting, Mr. Duggar," the guy said, choosing his words carefully. "But you know, Jesus, he talked to people one on one too. I think that's still vitally important today."

Apparently, Pops was frustrated by the pushback, so he tried a different angle and a new analogy.

"Just picture yourself in a stadium, and someone gives you a microphone." He let his words hang in the air for just a moment longer than necessary, as if the idea was so big and so magnificent that it needed extra time to compute. "You can speak to everyone in the stadium and tell them about the Lord. You'd take that opportunity in a heartbeat, wouldn't you? I mean, it's a no-brainer, right?"

The guy shifted awkwardly, wondering whether speaking the truth to power was worth it. He chose truth.

"I don't know, Mr. Duggar, sir. Not if God had told me to go and talk to the person under the bleachers. If I knew that the Lord wanted me to go talk to the one instead of the thousands, then I'd have to obey."

Pops froze. He looked like he'd just swallowed a fish bone. "Uh-uh," he said when he'd recovered himself, shaking his head. "No way. God would never tell you to do that."

When I heard the story, I was kind of stunned.

Was Pops really saying that he believed it was always God's desire for people to be involved in whichever ministry reached more people? And was he telling our friend that he knew God's will for this guy's life, and that it included filming? Was he really saying that to trust God's timing, we have to be able to see the results in our lifetime?

This was contrary to what Pops had always taught us kids. We'd grown up with him reminding us that, "Little is much when God is in it," and that "We don't always see how God is working." Yet Pops' words went directly against times in the Bible where Jesus broke away from large crowds to address or minister to one person. It left me feeling confused, and kind of sad.

Long before our family friend had questioned Pops like that, I had almost concluded that life would be easier if I just avoided the whole relationship thing for as long as I could. Like a lot of families within the IBLP world, there were plenty of rules (though we didn't like to call them that. My parents preferred "standards," "convictions," or "guidelines") and growing expectations about how us Duggar children would find a marriage partner. Instead of dating, we talked

Teenage Jill, late 2000s

about courtship, which was way more serious than simply playing around and having fun with people. We were only going to court someone we saw as a potential marriage partner, and we would always be chaperoned until the day we were married. We wouldn't kiss or even spend time alone in each other's company until we were married, and we wouldn't say "I love you" until we were officially courting and wouldn't hold hands until we were engaged. Only a guy could ask a girl to start courting, though if Pops (not Mom) felt like he wanted to encourage what he thought of as a good possible match between a guy and one of his daughters, it was okay for him to make hints and suggest we get to know each other.

Josh had navigated it all and gotten married when he was twenty, and I'd hoped that it wouldn't be too long before my Prince Charming would come along. But I knew I shouldn't let marriage constantly consume my thoughts. I also knew my parents loved me and wanted what was best for me, so it wasn't like Mom or Pops were ever going to actually arrange our marriages and force us to marry someone. But without our parents' blessing, there was simply no way that any relationship would ever be able to begin. Years and years of IBLP teaching had taught us that no good Christian child should consider going against our parents' wishes. Number one on the list of requirements in a future spouse was that we had the approval of our parents. Without that, it was game over before things had even begun.

We were encouraged not to just sit around waiting for our future mate to show up, but instead to occupy our time in ways that distracted us from constant thoughts of marriage. Mr. Gothard even taught that it was best to make a vow of single service, committing a specific number of years to serving God while single. His teaching

Joy, Jinger, Jessa, Jill, and Jana, 2014

was compelling, but I preferred to commit to serve God, my family, and others just until God brought my future husband along. I dressed conservatively, but inside I was a normal girl interested in romance and love like anyone else. I had desires and emotions, but I tried to keep them in check, and kept myself clear of the sin of talking about guys with my sisters. When we were younger, we were all encouraged to talk to our parents if we liked someone, asking them to help pray with us on it.

I was okay with waiting. As the show kept on rolling from one season to the next, my life was increasingly full. Not only did I have three young buddies to look after—Joy, James, and Jenni—but I was also training to be a midwife. Between filming, study, attending births, making sure that my three buddies were dressed, washed, fed, doing their schoolwork and everything else, trying not to think too much about finding Mr. Right wasn't too hard. Besides, Pops was already helping do some of the thinking for me.

By the time we'd wrapped up filming for season six, the show had gotten so popular that my parents were continually receiving requests for speaking engagements, meetings, and interviews. All of that attention led to Pops' opinion and advice being valued and sought after by lots of people. He often took calls with people seeking his counsel. Sometimes the calls were private, but there were times when he might invite a few of us kids to join him as he put the caller on speakerphone so we could listen in and hear them give an update of their ministry.

Duggar sisters at filmed family photo shoot

One morning before the film crew arrived, I was in the girls' bedroom getting ready with a few of my sisters when Pops wandered in, midway through a call. He muted it and quickly said, "There's a young man I've been talking to. His name is Derick and he's serving as a missionary in Nepal. Why don't y'all listen in for a while?"

I listened for a bit with my sisters, but I didn't want to seem too interested. Plus, I had errands to run, so I didn't pay too much attention.

The same thing happened about a month later, with Pops coming into the room that I was in and announcing that he was on a call with the missionary guy again, and again we listened to the conversation on speakerphone but didn't saying anything. This time after Pops got off the phone, he mentioned that Derick had a blog that we should look at some time. Something about the way Pops looked right at me as he spoke, told me that he had an agenda here.

Thinking maybe Pops was trying to set me up, I naturally avoided showing any deep interest. On one hand, I was twenty-one years old and had no desire to have my dad set me up with some random guy. In my opinion, that would be embarrassing and weird. Then again, I respected Pops, and there was just a small part of me that thought it was kind of sweet that he was looking out for me like this. So I decided to play along, listening carefully to what this missionary in Nepal guy had to say, but not give Pops any reason to suspect that I was interested.

Derick's life was different from mine. He was around my age, just a couple years older than me, and he came from the same corner of Arkansas, but while my days were filled with siblings and chores and TV crews, he had already graduated college and was out in Nepal, serving on the mission field. As he described some of the things he'd been doing since he and Pops last spoke—visiting remote Himalayan villages, building relationships with people who had probably never heard the gospel before—it sounded adventurous and exciting, especially as I'd been dreaming of going overseas and working full-time in mission work ever since my first out-of-country, short-term mission trip to Central America.

I wasn't about to get carried away though. When I next had some free time, I did a little research of my own, finding Derick's blog and Facebook page. There were a lot of nice photos and updates about the work he was doing, and he seemed like a decent guy. But I wasn't interested. I was too busy and focused on midwife schooling and clinicals, writing a book with my sisters, filming, and all the usual chores at home. My schedule was full.

The more Pops got to know Derick though, the more he liked him and the more eager he became, especially because we both had the calling to serve in full-time international missions. Pops started talking to me specifically about Derick, even suggesting that we might go visit him one day soon.

I didn't give it much thought, but my immediate reaction wasn't great. "It just seems a little awkward," I said. "I don't even know the guy!"

"Come on Jill," he said. "It'd be great. The network's talking about filming us on a vacation to Japan and China. When we're done, we could easily go visit him in Nepal before we fly home."

The trip was big news, a once-in-a-lifetime opportunity for sure. Even though we'd just been on a trip with the film crew two years before to Europe, I still wasn't used to this level of perks. I was still determined not to lose my head, so I played it cool and told Pops I'd check to see if the travel plans would work with my midwifery studies. It turned out they didn't, so while plans for the Japan and China trip went ahead, there was no chance of a Nepal swing.

Pops didn't push too much, but he was patiently persistent, and it wasn't long before another opportunity presented itself.

In March of 2013, we were on a road trip and were staying with friends in Illinois, when I stepped out from the house to grab something from our bus. Pops was in there, alone, phone pressed to his ear, smiling and talking with someone. As soon as he saw me, he motioned me over to sit down, flipping the call to speakerphone. It was Derick again, so I figured I knew how this was gonna go, with me listening quietly while Derick updated my dad on his work, just like the three or four times before. This time, however, Pops didn't keep my presence a secret.

"Hey Derick," he said when there was a pause. "I've got my daughter Jill here with me. Why don't you go ahead and tell her a little bit about yourself and your testimony."

Immediately my face was burning red. I mouthed, *You didn't tell me you were gonna do THAT! THIS IS SO EMBARRASSING!*, but Pops just smiled and waved me off. I dug him in the ribs with my elbow. Pops' grin just got bigger.

"Hey Jill," said Derick.

"Um, hey?" My voice was shaking like never before. "It's nice to meet you."

I was relieved when Derick took over the conversation. He told me a little about his upbringing—how he had just one sibling, how when he was just a freshman at Oklahoma State, his dad had died suddenly and how that had inspired him to get out and do something significant with his life. He talked about his time in Nepal, about how much he loved the mission field.

I didn't say much at all. Even if I'd had more questions, I didn't want to ask them right at that moment and egg on Pops' excitement. So I just listened, and in a few short minutes the conversation was over. Derick seemed like a kind person, but I wasn't interested in getting to know him. Instead, I just pushed the awkward telephone conversation out of my mind.

At first, way back in the early days when things were just getting going with the show, I was curious about being on TV. I wanted to see what it would be like, to observe what might come through the window of opportunity that God had created for us. As the show gathered momentum, my thoughts became clearer. People would often ask me how I felt about it all, typically assuming that I loved it, and that being on TV was the coolest thing ever. I'd always answer politely and try not to make anyone feel awkward, but their assumptions were wrong.

While it was cool at times, and we had some great adventures while filming the TV show, being on TV also had its downsides. As each season was filmed and aired, as more and more and more of Duggar family life was transmitted out to homes across the country, my opinion started to change. The more I experienced what it meant to allow your life to become the focus of a reality TV show, the more I understood that while it was still a ministry for Pops and the rest of us, it was something entirely different for the network that created us. The show—and by extension the entire Duggar family—was a vehicle for profit. No matter how much Pops talked about flying over NYC and the potential impact of reaching millions with the message of Christ, for the company paying the bills, we were there to entertain. We had to keep things fresh, and we knew that if we didn't provide the viewers with content they engaged with, there would be no show. If things ever got stale, it would be game over.

Keeping things fresh required a lot of planning and sometimes a little rehearsal. A guy asking Pops' permission to marry a Duggar girl, or the proposal itself, were some of the best TV moments, but there was practically no room for spontaneity. Each step would be rehearsed in advance. And sometimes, keeping things fresh meant bending the rules. So, even though physical contact between courting couples was banned, we'd be allowed to put our arms around each other if the show required it—which is exactly what happened in one episode that featured a weird triple date that involved some extravagant archery contest.

What I found the hardest, though, were the ways the show intruded on my most private moments. I was sixteen when I had surgery to remove my wisdom teeth—my first ever surgery. I hate needles and was anxious about everything that was involved in the procedure, and knowing that it was going to be the main focus of an episode only made things worse. But saying no to the cameras was not an option. The only comfort I could find was thinking about Mom. I knew she didn't like her birth being filmed, but she went along and did it anyway. If she put up with it, so should I.

The longer the show ran, the deeper we had to dig to keep

things fresh. Sometimes it was a matter of taking a trip overseas, like the mission trip to El Salvador in seasons two and five, or the epic journey to China and Japan after season six, or other trips to Israel, Britain, and Ireland. But we didn't have the budget or the time to fill the show with travel alone, and we had to look closer to home for new and exciting content. "There's no such thing as bad TV" was something the crew said so often that it became a family saying of our own, repeated whenever we encountered a minor crisis like an unplanned trip to the emergency room. Big life events were better, especially major milestones. Mom giving birth would always give our ratings a spike, but it wasn't the only life event that made for great TV. Whenever our producer, Scott, heard that one of us was going to start courting, his eyes would light up like a Christmas tree.

Derick and I had started talking regularly after the call on the bus, and the more we talked the more I liked him. So, inevitably I found myself sitting on the recliner chair in Mom and Pops' bedroom, facing my dad while I made a phone call to Scott and put him on speaker so we could both hear. I was feeling nervous, even though I knew I had Mom and Pops' full blessing. What I was about to say could not be unsaid. What I was about to do could not be undone.

"Scott? I have some news to share."

"Oh, really?"

"Yeah. I have a guy."

"What? Nice! Who?" He sounded excited and genuinely pleased for me, and for a moment I forgot that this was a business meeting.

"Yes, Scott. I have a guy. And he's in Nepal."

"Yes!" he said, sounding even more excited than before. Then he kinda laughed as he continued, "I don't know anything about this story or anything about this guy. But yes. Nepal's been on my bucket list since forever. When are we going?"

We all laughed. "Yeah, I totally did this for you, Scott."

I'd always liked Scott. He made filming fun, and I trusted him too. But I'd been doing the show long enough to understand the implications of what we were discussing.

"Scott, I've never met this guy before. We've only ever spoken on the phone or on Skype."

"Really? Oh. Well, that's even better. This is a great story, Jill."

"I know it is. But I have a question. If we go over there, and you film me meeting the guy for the first time, but it doesn't work out and we don't start courting, then do you have to air it? I just don't know how I'd feel putting that out there, and I wouldn't want to put this guy through it and all, either."

Scott's tone changed a bit. "I see what you're saying, but unfortunately, if we're going to make the investment of taking you, your dad and a crew over there, and taking all that time out of the regular filming schedule, then we'd have to air it regardless of how the relationship turns out. I'm sorry."

It was exactly the answer I'd feared.

I didn't wrestle with the decision for long—Scott needed an answer quickly—but I did wrestle hard. I liked Derick and had tried to explain what it meant to be in my reality TV family. I hated the thought of things not working out and having it broadcast all over the world. I could hardly think of anything more humiliating. Then again, this was my one shot at getting out to Nepal to see him. If I didn't take it, would that window of opportunity for me and Derick ever open again? I talked with Derick about the proposal too, since it would involve both of us.

In the end, the show won. I told Scott that I was willing to go. We found a couple of weeks in late November and made plans. Everything was looking good, for a while.

"Listen," he said over the phone when we were a month out from flying to Kathmandu. "We can't do two weeks over Thanksgiving. It's got to be five days."

"Excuse me?" I said. "You go for five days if you want, but if I'm going to decide whether this guy is someone I want to spend the rest

Derick and Jill on a motorcycle in Nepal

of my life with, I need two weeks. I'll do whatever you want. We can film a pretend goodbye scene and I'll turn on the tears for you, but I'm not doing this in five days. I just can't."

That time, I won. The crew filmed Pops and I during our two days of travel from northwest Arkansas to Nepal, as well as mine and Derick's first meeting—a moment that I wished could have been private. They then stayed another five days filming various things around Kathmandu. Just before we faked our goodbyes for the show, Derick asked me on-camera if I would be willing to start an official courtship. My yes was 100 percent straight from the heart.

Derick asking Jill to begin official courtship during departure scene in Nepal

Jill and Derick in Nepal after the film crew left

I was so thankful for that extra week we got to spend together without the film crew. We were able to get to know each other better, and over the days there were little snatched moments when Pops gave us space and our feelings grew. Like the evening when Pops was chaperoning us in the room that he and I were sharing, but he ended up falling asleep. Derick and I sat on the end of the bed eating hot chicken fried rice out of makeshift tinfoil bowls that Derick had grabbed from a street vendor. We talked about everything and nothing, and when it was time to go, Derick looked at me.

"Goodnight," he said. "I love you."

"Goodnight," I said. "I love you too."

* * *

I fell deeply in love with Derick. He was polite and respectful, and I could see that Pops was genuinely impressed with him. So when it was *really* time to go, I was so sad to leave. I cried on his shoulder when I said goodbye in the car at the airport, and then I cried a few more times on the long trip home.

The good news was that Derick's two-year term on the mission field was almost up, so a couple of months later he returned to Arkansas. (He was gracious when his closest friends were forced to wait downstairs at the airport so that the crew could film my family welcoming him by himself first!) I wasn't surprised that the rest of the Duggar family soon got to know and love him too. He impressed my parents by quickly landing a full-time job doing tax accounting at Walmart HQ, as well as enrolling in a seminary class, and everybody who met him told me how kind and genuine he was. Every time I heard those words, I could feel myself sighing with relief. I'd found a guy who I was in love with, who my parents approved of, and who wasn't going to cause tension within the family or have a problem with filming. Derick was unique, and there was no way I was letting him go.

Derick came back to the US in January 2014, but by the end of February we were already talking about getting married. At the end of March, Derick proposed—successfully working with Scott and the crew to deliver all the ingredients of a great episode—and we started planning our June wedding.

It was Easter Sunday when Derick called and told me that his mom had been diagnosed with non-Hodgkin's lymphoma.

Jill meeting Derick at the airport when
he returned from Nepal, January 2014

"It's stage four," he said. "The first doctor she saw wasn't even willing to treat her and told her there was nothing they could do at this point. She found another doctor who gave her a second opinion and he is going to start intense chemo next week. But they haven't given her much hope."

I was in Hot Springs, Arkansas, four hours away, chaperoning Jessa as she spent time with the guy she was courting. I felt the earth shattering all around me. Derick's mom and I had become very close

friends over the last several months, and she'd told me how excited she was to finally be getting a daughter. I couldn't imagine what Derick was going through, having already lost his dad, and now being told that his mom was likely going to die too. He'd be left with just one sibling, and I couldn't even begin to comprehend what that must have felt like. Whenever I tried to put myself in that position, the feeling of loneliness was so terrifying that it made it hard to breathe.

But Derick was not like me. As the days and weeks rolled by, I was witness to the strength of his character, the depth of his faith, and the power of the bonds of love that held his family together. He continued to work, to check in on his mom and help her where needed, supporting his wonderful stepdad Ronnie who was caring for her 24/7. Derick continued to attend seminary, plan the wedding, and still make himself available for filming. His determination and capacity for hard work was awe-inspiring, and the more I got to know his mom, Cathy, the more it made sense. She received her cancer diagnosis with courage and the kind of wholehearted trust in God that takes a lifetime to mature. She refused to give in to fear and told everyone who asked how she was feeling that she was convinced she was going to survive.

Cathy's diagnosis meant that the wedding was even more significant on a personal level. For a while at least, the fact that the day would be filmed and broadcast took a back seat. That didn't last long. I was the first Duggar daughter to get married, and the network was determined to get as much great TV out of it as possible. As the big day got closer, more and more of the decisions were made with the show in mind.

Most of the time I was okay with it. I didn't mind that the guest list had grown to two thousand, or that some of them were complete strangers to me. I didn't care. I was focused on getting through the wedding planning details and marrying my best friend. But when it came to the photos, we had a problem.

I wanted all the guests to be able to take photos and then share them on an app with special tags so I could have copies of all their pictures. The network did not agree.

"They want exclusive rights," said Pops, "and they're worried that if we let people take photos, they'll leak. They're offering to pay for photographers."

I was tired and stressed and for a while I tried to dig in and hold my ground—in the sweetest, most polite way possible. But my holding out didn't last. The pressure mounted.

"This is not a hill to die on," said Derick after the subject had come up at a wedding planning meeting we'd had with my dad and another representative from the network. "We can let this one go." Reluctantly, I agreed with him.

The whole month leading up to the wedding was a blur, but I was still aware that some changes were happening. There was talk of a new season of the show being agreed on. Also, Pops hired somebody to work with him for the first time ever, which struck me as notably different, but good. The show had grown in popularity, and my parents were both getting pretty overwhelmed by things. Pops had always kept things to himself, but there had been times when I'd wondered whether it was all starting to get a little too much for him. So it made sense for them to get some help. Bringing in this new guy, Chad, to help with public relations and any negotiations or business deals could only be a good thing.

Then there was the plane. The higher our viewer numbers had climbed, the more time Mom and Pops had been spending traveling to different speaking engagements. It had started to get a little too much for them, so Pops bought a four-seater, single-engine plane and arranged for a local pilot friend to fly them when they needed to travel. Being Pops, and knowing my brother John's childhood dream to become a pilot, he also arranged for this friend to give John flight lessons, so John often accompanied them on flights to gain training hours. I was happy for my parents and John, and though I thought about it briefly, I didn't want to ask how much the plane had cost or where the money had come from.

And then, eight days before the wedding, at our final planning meeting, Derick received a call.

Jill and Derick doing interviews at the shop

We were all at a local restaurant—Derick and I, Mom, Pops, Jana, all three of my wedding coordinator friends. Derick and I had just come from seeing his mom at the hospital, but before we could even start the meeting, Derick's phone rang and he stepped away from the table.

He didn't say much on the call, just a few basic questions. I watched the blood drain from his face.

When it was finished, he pocketed his phone, walked back, and looked at everyone. "I'm sorry. I think I've got to go. My mom's gotten worse. She's being Life Flighted by helicopter to a new hospital. She's not doing well. It sounds pretty serious."

In that moment, everything changed. For weeks my phone had been constantly announcing some new message to respond to, a

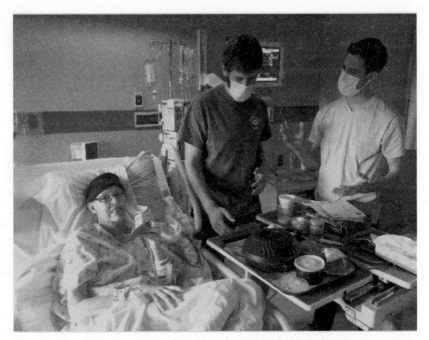

Derick's brother, Dan, and Derick with Cathy in the hospital, June 2014

missed call to return or some vital decision that was long overdue. I no longer had the capacity to deal with it. If it hadn't been for my sister Jana offering to take my phone and handle all the wedding stuff for me in the final days, I'd have spun out completely.

I spent those days leading up to the wedding visiting the hospital as much as possible. Whenever we were not there, I fully expected Derick to receive another call at any moment telling him to get back and be with his mom before she passed. I was braced for impact, my insides clenched, my heart just moments away from breaking.

But the call never came.

The day before our wedding, we'd started to hope that Derick's mom might actually make it. She was even talking about joining us at the church. "Mom says she's going to be there," said Derick. "I don't know how, but they're saying they will let her sign a release and let her out of the hospital on oxygen to be there."

It was the best news ever, and I hoped and prayed she would be able to make it. The day was a blur, with the Big House full of people, and the levels of noise and chaos and laughter higher than ever. After I ran by the hospital to check on Cathy, I rushed back home to move some of my things out, then got ready for the filmed wedding rehearsal run-through at the church that after-noon, followed by the rehearsal dinner that evening. My brothers were excited to be heading out with Derick to his bachelor party after the dinner that evening, and my older sisters and I were like a bunch of giggling preteens once again, as we were going to stay at a hotel for some extra sister time away from the chaos. Overall it was a good day, but one memory stands out more in hindsight than the others.

"Hey," said Pops to some of the older siblings earlier in the day. "Chad and I have been finalizing stuff on the new show, and I have some papers for y'all to sign here. Can you do it real quick before you leave?"

"Sure," I said, not thinking much about it. Some of the big TLC and production people who weren't usually around were coming to town, so I imagined Pops was feeling more pressure than normal to get everything they needed together. "What's this for?"

"Oh, it's just about how you're gonna get paid."

I looked at the papers sitting on the dining room table—single sheets with signature lines with each of our names printed. A few had already been signed. I didn't see any extra papers to read, and I didn't really know what it was about, but I didn't question my dad. After all, in all my life, I'd never had reason not to trust Pops. He knew best, and always had.

So I picked up the pen and signed.

CHAPTER FOUR

Costs

Two hours before the wedding ceremony was due to start—just after we'd done an on-the-fly interview with *People* magazine—Derick and I were able to spend a few precious moments together, alone. We fed each other Chick-fil-A nuggets and tried to keep the grease off our clothes. It was a precious moment, made even more special by a call Derick received about his mom. Cathy was coming to the wedding. She'd be in a wheelchair, on oxygen, and would be accompanied by a nurse who would help make sure that she kept her distance from people in order to avoid catching germs, but she was coming. Waves of relief and gratitude flooded over me.

The ceremony made my already full heart even more emotional. I wanted to be present, to soak up every moment, every feeling. The beauty of the music we had chosen, the smiles on the faces of so many people that I loved, the power of the vows we took, the

Jill and Derick on their wedding day, June 21, 2014

tenderness of my first-ever kiss. Sometimes I just had to pause and remind myself to breathe.

The rest of the day had all the typical wedding day chaos, with the added features of a camera crew, multiple official photographers and uninvited paparazzi lurking outside, but I tried to block out the noise caused by the show.

When you're in the world of reality TV, everything has a cost. The shopping carts full of great food, the trip to Nepal to meet Derick in person for the first time, the wedding itself—they all came with a price tag, which we paid by letting the cameras into our lives, giving them access to all the raw, unfiltered action to be served up as entertainment. Don't get me wrong, it was a privilege to be able to benefit like that. Being a Duggar on TV meant that I had opportunities and experiences that I would never have enjoyed otherwise. The show gave me so much, and I am grateful for the places I have been, the moments I have enjoyed, and the people I have met.

But . . .

. . . some things are not worth the cost. Some things are not for sale.

In among all the emotional turbulence that we were going through in the run-up to the wedding, I was always clear our honeymoon would not be on the show. It was private and it was precious, and it was absolutely not something that I was willing to sell for an all-expenses-paid honeymoon vacation. I'd seen what had happened when Josh and his bride, Anna, had let the network pay for their honeymoon to South Carolina—how they'd edited it in a way that made the two of them appear like inexperienced, naïve kids who had grown up in a sheltered environment and were about to head off to have sex for the first time. The whole thing was embarrassing and designed to make them look bad. I didn't want that for Derick and me.

There was only a little pushback from the production team, but once we made it clear we weren't taking cameras along on our honeymoon, they made it clear there wasn't any money from them to help with the honeymoon either. We took five days and disappeared off to the beach in North Carolina. It suited us to keep it simple and short. Our bank balance was low, Derick only had a few days' vacation available, and with Cathy back home, still on edge recuperating from the wedding day, we were worried about even being away at all.

We returned to confusion and surprised looks on the faces of the friends of Pops who were working on the house he was flipping—our first home as a married couple.

"What are you guys doing back so soon?"

"Aren't you supposed to be on your honeymoon?"

"We figured you'd be away the whole month."

I thought about trying to explain the challenges of Derick's work schedule and the fact that we were living on a budget, but decided not to. Cathy was getting better, Derick and I had just begun the application process to serve as missionaries, and I was just a few months away from my final exams to become a midwife. My life as a married woman of twenty-three was finally beginning. This was a time for looking forward, not back.

A few days after we got back from our honeymoon it was like we'd never been away. TLC wanted the episodes featuring the wedding to air as soon as possible, so Scott and his guys were up against a crazy tight deadline to get all the interviews shot. Pops had recently converted one of the shops at the front of the Big House into a studio, so we only had to drive thirty minutes from where we lived in Rogers, but even so, with Derick working forty-five hours a week as a manager at the Walmart home office with a team that handled the company's tax audits, the only time we could film was in the evenings and on weekends. I felt bad bringing him into all this, but he had a good attitude about it, and I hardly heard him complain.

It was days after the wedding when he received a call from his mom Cathy, who was due to have a scan that day, to see whether the first of six planned rounds of chemo had made any impact. I'd been praying nonstop. But as the phone rang and Derick set it on speaker, I couldn't help feeling the fear start to knot up my stomach.

"I've got news," she said. "You know that chemo nearly killed me, don't you?"

Derick shot me a worried look. "Yes, Mom."

"Well, it didn't. But it looks like it killed the cancer. Doc says I'm cancer free. Said he didn't know how, but that it must have been some kind of miracle." She broke off, laughing. "I told him that prayer works."

It was the best news ever.

Then, on a Sunday evening, when we'd been married just a month, I had more news to get excited about. I found out I was pregnant.

I was tired and not doing so well with the morning sickness, and Derick was trying to throw himself into work, but there was little time to relax. Most days when Derick finished work, we'd have filming to do, and there was even more to get through most weekends. Evenings were the worst, and the crew would often wind up a little frustrated with us if we were running late or if Derick took more than a few minutes to eat some food and get changed.

"Hey guys," Scott would shout from downstairs whenever they were filming at our house. "Come on now. Time's running out. We don't want to run late again."

I can understand why it was annoying for the crew to have to wait for us, and they probably had no idea that we had never been paid for our filming and were working as volunteers. I'd never questioned it, because that's the way it had always been, right from the start. And I had always been warned not to talk about the show's inner workings or details with anyone for as long as I could remember. Plus, I would not want to hint at or say anything that could potentially be negative toward my parents either. We were just kids when the show first started, and all we knew was that it was Pops' show, and our job was to do what was asked of us. To my way of thinking back then, asking to be paid for appearing on the show would have been as crazy as asking to be paid for helping build the Big House.

It was different now that Derick and I were married, and the twenty hours of filming we had to fit in each week quickly became a burden for us. If we were lucky, we'd have it wrapped up by

Filming the guys' pre-wedding getaway one month after the wedding, July 2014

nine p.m. Other times, we'd still be filming at midnight. Ironically, this "family filming ministry," which emphasized putting your family first, was sucking the life out of ours.

We both treasured any moments that we had for ourselves, where no camera crew could tell us to hurry up. I chose to drive Derick to and from work every day that I could, and those conversations in the car became our safe space, a place where we could talk honestly about the stresses of the day.

It didn't take long for the subject of the show to come up.

"All this filming," said Derick as we drove away from the house at six thirty one morning. "It's hard."

We drove a little farther in silence. Between the pregnancy nausea and the shivers of anxiety caused by my old need for approval, I kept quiet.

"And with you being pregnant and all, it's even harder. Is it always like this?"

"I know. I'm finding it hard too. But just a little longer. Once Jessa gets married and starts having kids, maybe it will lighten our load a little and be easier for us then."

Derick thought awhile.

"You know what I wish?"

"No."

"That we could say 'this doesn't work for us,' and they'd make a change."

A fresh wave of nausea hit me. "Oh babe, we can't rock the boat. Not like that. Not this soon after we got married."

For a moment I wondered whether Derick was going to say something else. But he paused, looked at me and reached for my hand.

"I love you," he said, squeezing it in time with each word.

"I love you too," I said. Four squeezes.

Like all good IBLP parents, Mom and Pops believed their adult children—even those of us who were married and starting to have families of their own—were still under their parental authority. We were careful to avoid their displeasure, and so pretty much did whatever was expected of us, from wearing the right clothes to saying yes to whatever the show required. So while we'd been able to hold our ground and keep our honeymoon private, when it came to announcing that I was pregnant, there was no chance of us calling the shots. Josh and his wife Anna had three kids by the time Derick and I married, and Mom had given birth six times already since we started filming, so there was already a clear path that we had to follow—not just involving some media outlet being given exclusive rights to the official announcement, but also how we told those closest to us. First, we were supposed to tell the producers, then—when they were ready to capture it on film—we were allowed to tell our parents. I bent the rules a little, telling a couple of my sisters and buddies first, but when it came time to tell my parents and Derick's mom and stepdad, I made sure I followed the rules.

I had to promise the crew that we would all keep it a secret if I went ahead and told them, since we couldn't make a formal announcement for another month—due to the show still rolling out our wedding story and teasing the blossoming relationship and forthcoming wedding of my sister Jessa and Ben. So a few days after we found out, with cameras rolling, we took a trip over to the Big House and told my family. At first it was just the way I'd imagine it would be for any other family. The room was full of excitement and laughter and a little sibling teasing along the lines of "You're gonna get so fat!" and "Derick's gonna love those diaper changes." It was normal and fun, and I could feel myself wanting to inhale every moment of it.

A day or so later, the spell broke.

I was inundated with emails, texts, and calls from the network and production crew as they were trying to organize things and make sure "the announcement"—carefully scheduled so as not to detract from Jessa's wedding—went off without a hitch. Everyone said they were excited for us. I was tempted to remind people that this was my baby we were talking about, but I didn't want to play the role of Crabby First-Time Mom. Not yet at least.

TLC's talent management informed us that *People* magazine would have the rights to the story, and that they were going to schedule a photoshoot in the coming days. We couldn't tell anyone other than a small group of family and friends until *People* broke the story, and even then, we'd have to coordinate precisely with them for the birth announcement of our own child.

We were six years into the show and a little more than one month married, and although I hadn't been the one pregnant before, I was kind of used to the timeline and rules, so not much of what they said surprised me. But as I relayed the information to Derick that evening, I could see the confusion in his eyes.

"So we cannot tell a single other soul, and those we've told already we have to get to swear to absolute secrecy," he said, re-capping what I'd just told him. "When it's the day to announce, the magazine gets to post it on their site first. And then, two hours later, we can repost on our social media, just sharing our excitement and telling people to read the full story online or in print from *People* magazine and remind them to tune in to TLC to see more. So basically, we get to announce the announcement, right?"

"Right."

"And this is normal?"

"Yeah."

"But this isn't normal. This is insane, Jill! I don't like being a dancing monkey who has to perform at these stupid photo shoots. And I don't like having to bend to the demands of when and how we're going to post our own family announcements!"

Derick's demeanor was controlled, but I could tell he was very upset at the restrictions. He started throwing out some ideas, like going rogue and posting our own pregnancy announcement. But as a good IBLP girl who obeyed her dad, I knew that was a big no-no. I tried to rein him back in again.

"Babe, we can't just post our own family announcements. TLC and my dad would be furious."

"So we're basically slaves of TLC and your dad. Is that how it is?!" Then Derick paused in his frustration. "If it's this intense around the announcement, what's it going to be like with the birth?"

I knew the answer, but I didn't want to tell him. Mom had learned how to manage the expectations of the show when it came to giving birth—allowing them access but being firm about what shots they were allowed to take. Josh's wife, Anna, had had problems with the crew using footage from one of her births that she'd specifically told them she did not authorize. They cut it out for reruns, but with later births, the footage was often added back in as part of flashback sequences.

I felt terrible for Anna and my mom for being made to feel like they had to give up control of their labors like that. It seemed like their only consolation was the fact that this was part of a God-given ministry. It was a big cost to pay.

For me, in those early months of pregnancy, I tried not to think about birth too much. I wanted to please everyone, but it didn't seem possible. On one hand I wanted to make Derick happy and totally agreed with him about not wanting to hand over control of the pregnancy and birth to the network. However, according to IBLP teaching, Derick was also under my parents' authority and was supposed to obey them too.

Even though I was now Mrs. Jill Dillard, I was still Sweet Jilly Muffin. I wanted to please everyone, not just my husband, but my parents and the network as well. I was a mess of conflict and didn't know how to balance the feelings. All I really knew for sure was that if I messed up and didn't get my parents' blessing, I would be sinning by not following God's will.

Just when life was threatening to get a little too intense, the clouds parted. Pops announced that he was taking a bunch of Duggars on a week-long mission trip back down to El Salvador in December 2014, and invited Derick and me to join them. Neither of us had to think long before we said yes. Even though it would be a pretty busy trip with less than desirable amenities, especially considering I was going to be nearing my final trimester, it sounded like a nice break from some of the chaos and long workdays back home. The irony of seeking comfort and respite from the stresses of life in El Salvador, which of course had its own very hard stresses and circumstances, wasn't lost on either of us.

Derick had spent two years in Nepal, and he'd traveled widely throughout Asia, but he'd never been to Latin America before. I was excited to show him the project that my family had visited several times over the previous years, and I had a hunch that he'd fall in love with the friends, the food, the scenery, and the children there just as much as I had.

It was everything I'd hoped it would be.

Those five days were a pause on everything that was making life at home stressful. My morning sickness had finally eased, and for once, there was no conflict between our schedule and the rest of the Duggar family's. It was a relief to not feel like we were letting people down or making life difficult for them.

But better than all of that was the chance to see Derick in action. He didn't mind the heat, the lack of creature comforts, the chance to serve others, and the opportunities to sit and talk with people about life, God, and everything else. I'd only been able to see a little of this in Nepal, and it was a privilege to witness him come alive like this in El Salvador.

The trip was full of great moments. Sleeping on an air mattress on the front porch of the church, playing Mary and Joseph in the nativity story performed at church, spending time together without the pressure of filming. But the best of all was seeing Derick interact with the kids at the orphanage. His mom was adopted, and it meant so much to see the kids' faces light up when he and some of the other team members played soccer with them and goofed around.

The day before we flew back home, we were riding in the truck with Mike, the director of missions. He was telling us how they had started working with ex–gang members, providing them with food, job training and pastoral support, when he asked us a question that I didn't see coming.

"We could use a young couple like you down here, helping support the growing local church ministry and coming alongside Indigenous leaders to provide jobs in gang communities, which would help people stay out of the gangs. Would you pray about coming down and working with us? It would only be for a year initially, maybe two."

I was stunned. But I was also intrigued. Derick and I exchanged glances, and I knew he felt the same too.

A month later, after we'd prayed and sought counsel from people we trusted—including my parents and Derick's mom—we called Mike up and told him that we were in, pending some things. We explained that we wanted to wait a few more months before we moved, which would allow me to give birth in April and make sure everything went well with me and the baby. Mike was happy, and Derick and I were pumped. Those morning and evening car conversations on the way to and from his work were now focused less on the stress of filming, and more on this new adventure that our little family was about to embark upon.

The closer we got to April and my due date, the more I thought about what the show might want from the birth. Both Mom and Anna had let the cameras in for all their births, but I wasn't so sure

Jill with Derick as Pistol Pete at an OSU
basketball game for the show, February 2015

myself. My midwifery training had exposed me to what could go wrong, and I knew myself well enough to know that in that most intimate, vulnerable place of childbirth, I'd value my privacy more than ever. But keeping the cameras out just didn't seem possible.

When I first raised this with Derick, he didn't see a problem. "We can just tell them what we want to do," he said.

"Babe, no. You don't understand. That's not how this is. We cannot just tell them what we do and don't want."

Derick frowned. "But this isn't like an engagement or a birth announcement. This is *birth* . . . ," He left it hanging.

"Yeah," I said. "But . . . they have certain expectations."

We came back to the conversation a few times, but it always felt like we got stuck in the same place. Derick couldn't understand how the show could just assume so much power over the birth, and—after more than a decade in front of the cameras—I couldn't imagine how we could ever hope to stand up for what we wanted. We were stuck in a loop, and the birth was getting closer.

In the end, Scott brought it up one evening after we'd finished filming. It was just him and us in the house—no Pops, no Chad—which felt like the best possible way to start.

"So," he began, like a chef describing a meal he was planning. "Here's what we're thinking about the birth. TLC really wants to do it well, so we're talking about a couple of one-hour specials. One will be a quick turnaround show that will air within a week of the birth if all goes as planned. For that one we will have all the lead-up already shot, with a place held at the end where we'll just drop in a few minutes of the delivery before it airs. And then there will be the other special, which will be a more extensive telling of the birth in the follow-up episode that will likely air about three weeks after the birth. How does that sound, guys?"

I breathed deep to calm myself, just like I'd seen many mamas, doulas, and midwives do. "I just don't feel comfortable with filming the birth, Scott. As a student midwife, I feel like I already have some anxiety about the birth itself because I know too much, and I know I'm going to be up in my head. On top of that, I don't want to feel like a watched pot."

Scott sat back. "Okay," he said, as he wrestled with the puzzle. "How about we do what we did for Anna's last two? I'll just be outside with a camera, and I'll come in and get a shot here and there whenever you want me to."

Another breath. Even deeper this time. "No. I really don't even want that, Scott. I don't want it filmed."

At that, Scott started tearing up. He'd been with the show almost since the beginning, and we'd been through a lot together. He'd traveled everywhere we had and had shared all our significant moments. He was Uncle Scott, and I felt horrible talking to him like this. Somewhere, though, there was just a small part of me that wondered if he was tearing up because of the pressure that TLC was putting on him to get us to agree to him filming the birth.

"It's not you, Scott. You're great. It's me. If I'm tense, I won't be able to push this baby out."

"Okay," he said, sitting up straight. The mood had shifted. I knew the dance. Whatever came next would be his final offer. "What if we give you some cameras? Your mom and Jana will be there, right?"

I nodded. This was his last offer—the compromise I had to make. If I said no to my mom and sister shooting home video, I'd have an even bigger battle on my hands. Pops and the whole network would probably get involved. I didn't know whether Derick and I could withstand a force like that.

All my plans for a natural birth went up in smoke when I was in my third day of labor. Once my water broke, I tried to get the labor going at home with the midwife. It would start for a while but kept stopping. After more than forty hours of this, we decided to go to the hospital. Another twenty-four hours followed, first with Pitocin, then an epidural, but still no baby. In fact, after the epidural, the baby got himself into an undeliverable position known as breech transverse—just him chilling in a hammock-type position. I was exhausted. So, after laboring for sixty-eight hours straight, Israel David Dillard was finally brought into this world by C-section on April 6, 2015. Between all the drugs I was on, and the gowns and screens and bright lights required for the surgical procedure, Scott ended up getting a whole lot more footage from my mom and Jana's cameras than he'd probably thought he would—a lot more than if the labor had proceeded at home as planned, naturally and simply in a birth pool in my bedroom. But he didn't get everything. Derick had his own video camera with him, and we'd agreed that whatever he captured would only ever be just for us.

As I sat in my hospital bed, staring in awe at this beautiful baby boy as he nursed, I was aware that my brain was pretty fogged up with all those post-labor hormones. I was like an astronaut who'd landed back on earth, still unsure of what I'd just been through. But I was able to think clearly enough to be worried that Derick was going to fail to follow the plan that Chad and the network had laid out to us for the birth—*People* magazine was going to announce first, and as a family we would only use whatever photos they approved. If any pictures or news leaked, we'd be in trouble.

Between the fear of not meeting all the network's wishes, keeping the story from getting out prematurely, and the guilt about our personal secret videoing of the birth, I felt like I might have been rebelling against Pops, and I wasn't sure how that sat with me. Even though all the conversations about the show's access to my labor had been between me and Scott and Derick, I knew that nearly everything

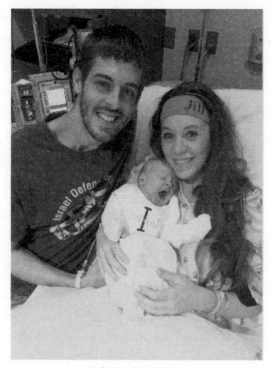

Baby Israel, April 2015

we'd discussed would have been shared with Pops, especially when it caused a problem. The show was still his show, and even though his kids were growing up, getting married, and having babies of their own, we were still the source of many of those great TV moments that kept the ratings high. More than that, even though I was a married woman and now a mama of my own, I was still my father's daughter. When he said he was giving me to Derick at the wedding altar, it was an empty gesture. IBLP teaching was clear that his authority over me would never diminish. If I disobeyed him or didn't honor his wishes and stepped out from under the umbrella of protection, I would be exposing myself to potential harm.

I was blind to it at the time, but eventually I would see just how dangerous and toxic IBLP's teachings about authority were in my life. The umbrella principle had sounded harmless enough when I was a child, but it was a brutally effective means of instilling fear and controlling behavior in the lives of others, regardless of whether they were adults or children. The fear of what would happen if I stepped out from under this umbrella had bled into every part of my life, and it left me second-guessing so many decisions. Even hiding a camera from Scott in the hope that I might be able to preserve my modesty and prevent the whole world from seeing me give birth felt like a risk. My father wanted us to cooperate with the show, therefore deceiving Scott could be seen as an act of sinful rebellion against my father if he disagreed. I could be outside the umbrella, and then something terrible might happen.

I was stressing about Derick, worrying that he might do or say something that would upset Scott, but he followed the plan to the letter. For the sake of our marriage, he stepped under the umbrella with me, even though he later told me how weird, and somewhat angry, he felt when the first photo he ever saw of Israel was when Pops stepped out of my hospital room and showed him the picture that he was about to send to Chad for *People* magazine.

We settled into our new life, enjoying our new baby as much as possible between filming as we prepared to depart for El Salvador. Summer was only weeks away, our first anniversary was approaching fast, and we were learning to let ourselves flow in time with the rhythms of a newborn baby. Even the guilt around keeping things from Scott and Pops started to fade.

And then one evening in May 2015, Derick and I were around at the Big House when Pops came into the room, looking drained and worried. He looked like he'd forgotten how to hold the smile that he wore so often.

He gathered some of us older ones around and spoke softly, choosing his words like he was picking a route through a minefield.

"I just got word that a tabloid has information about stuff that happened a long time ago. Stuff that happened between Josh and the girls."

I was in shock. Nobody spoke. We all just waited for Pops to continue.

"*In Touch* magazine has been able to get a copy of the police report from the investigation. I don't know how they got it, but I'm told that the information it contains is graphic."

Nobody breathed.

Silence.

"I'm doing all that I can to make them stop. I'm sure that what they're doing is illegal, and I want to get this nipped in the bud."

The rest of the evening was a blur. My head was spinning. All I wanted was to get back home and close the doors and windows and forget all about everything that had happened. I wanted to dig a hole so big that none of these memories could ever reach the surface again. And if that didn't work, I hoped that somehow, Pops would be able to shut this down.

I barely slept, but when I did my dreams were full of shadows and fear.

The only steady source of peace I could find was watching Israel as he fed or slept. I didn't think I could love him any more than I did the day he was born, but as everything threatened to explode outside, watching my beautiful boy steadied my heart.

When daylight came, there was no point hiding. Derick needed to get to work, and I had a doctor's appointment scheduled. Because I wasn't yet fully recovered from my C-section, I couldn't lift Israel in his car seat, so Jessa came over to take me to the appointment. I was glad for that. It felt like a day to have your sister by your side.

On the way to the appointment, I tried to distract myself, to live in the present and think about what else I needed to accomplish that day. I told myself that everything was just fine, but there was a knot in my stomach, a cord tied tight around my throat. At times I felt like the air was running out.

We had just parked and Jessa was about to get Israel out of the back of the car when Pops called.

"They've released it. I'm sorry."

Immediately, Jessa and I burst into tears.

"They promised us secrecy," I said when I could finally speak. "They said it was private. That it was a safe place. How could this happen?"

I was in shock all afternoon. I couldn't believe that what I had told people in confidence at the Child Safety Center all those years ago had been released. I could easily remember how much it had cost me to talk about what had happened with Josh—how painful it had been to dredge up those memories, and how frightened I was that we would be taken away from my parents as a result. How could anyone involved in that process be willing to release it to the media?

The state of shock didn't last for long. Like a landslide thundering down a valley after a night of storms, there was worse to come.

For when I finally summoned the courage to visit the *In Touch* website and read the story for myself, I was instantly engulfed by a deep, all encompassing, overwhelming sense of horror.

They had published everything. All the details from the investigation—details that we had shared in hushed whispers with tear-filled eyes—were now splashed across the screen. But it wasn't only presented in the cold, forensic language of the initial report. This was tabloid journalism at its worst. The most graphic, the most scandalous, the most painful parts of the story had received the greatest prominence. It was written with one aim and one aim only: entertainment.

As soon as I heard Derick's key in the lock that evening, I ran to him. He held me tight and cried along with me. I'd told him about the abuse back when we were nearly engaged, a little more than a year earlier. The release of the report was salt on an already open wound for him, and he was angry. It took all his self-control to stay calm for me.

"Hey. How're you doin'?"

"Terrible," I said. I'm an avoider by nature, but there was no hiding from this. The weight was enough to crush me. "I wish I were dead."

That was all there was to say. I couldn't speak much more. I just cried.

The nightmares started that night. It had been over a decade since the initial abuse, and until that point I'd never dreamed about what had happened. But as soon as *In Touch* published the story, the trauma started to replay itself in my dreams.

Daylight didn't offer much relief.

The doorbell rang soon after Derick went to work, and I didn't think twice at first about who it might be or what they might want. I peeked out like I normally would, saw an unexpected package on the ground and someone leaving, walking right by the network's security guard who had let him through. I paused, watching the delivery guy return to his car, pull out a camera with a long lens and train it on the front door. I looked closer. There were more of them.

They stayed there all day. All I could do to defend myself from them was keep the blinds down and try to stay out of the yard, which was easily visible from the road. I was trapped. I wanted to go hide under a rock. I had spent my entire life being taught that modesty was so important and that it was my responsibility as a godly woman not to behave or dress in a way that would cause any man to have impure thoughts. And now the whole world was able to read about—and imagine—what happened to me. I felt naked, ashamed, humiliated. I was being paraded through the streets, my sexual abuse being served up as nothing more than entertainment.

I spent a lot of time on the phone that morning. I talked to my sisters, to my parents, to Cathy and to Derick, too, when he was able to get a break. They were all loving and supportive, and I was grateful for them all. We were all struggling together.

Talking with people I trusted didn't take away the feelings of humiliation and shame that I was experiencing, but it did help to clarify who I held accountable for all this: the chief of police at the time, Kathy O'Kelley; the city of Springdale and its attorney, Ernest

Cate; Washington County Sheriff's Office, and its major sheriff, Rick Hoyt. The magazine itself, *In Touch*, and its parent company Bauer, plus any other unnamed players.

In the months and years that followed, a lot of people have shared their opinions on how I responded to the releasing of the report. Some offered their support and their understanding, and I am grateful to them. But others have accused me of blaming the wrong people. They said I was covering for my parents, that it was Mom and Pops' fault that all this happened in the first place.

It wasn't and I'm not.

I hold Josh responsible for his actions.

And I hold *In Touch*, Bauer, Kathy O'Kelley, Ernest Cate, the city of Springdale, the Washington County Sheriff's Office and Rick Hoyt responsible for illegally releasing and publishing the report— for inflicting on me and my sisters the trauma of a second victimization, a trauma that was made so much worse than the first by the fact that it was so public.

I am clear about the mistakes that my parents have made over the years with our upbringing, especially Pops, but the way my parents handled or didn't handle things with Josh does not influence or justify the release of juvenile records and further re-traumatization and exploitation of innocent victims.

The paparazzi were everywhere. Whenever we left the house they'd follow us in their cars, lenses trained on us like snipers. They tried to get to Derick at work, and there were a ton of them camped out at the Big House. A friend of Pops' offered for everyone to go and stay at his ranch in Oklahoma, so my family decamped there in the hope of peace.

Derick and I visited on the weekend. I could feel myself exhale as soon as we turned off the road and onto the property. It was peaceful out there at the ranch, surreal to be in a place of such tranquility when everything else in our world was being dominated by trauma. But while the ranch was free from paparazzi, it couldn't banish the pressure from our family. As soon as we stepped into the cabin that had become Duggar HQ, I could feel the tension.

The family was spread around the room. Some were playing board games, others about to go out for a walk. Mom was with the littlest ones, and Pops was in the corner with Chad, his right-hand man.

Josh and his family were also there. This might seem strange, but I suppose events were somehow viewed as a "thing of the past" by that point. It had been about three months since I'd last seen Josh. He'd moved to Washington, DC, in 2013 to work for a conservative group lobbying against access to things like stem-cell research, abortion, divorce, and pornography (ironically enough, given later events). As soon as the story broke, he resigned and he, Anna, and the kids all fled the paparazzi and came back to Arkansas.

I didn't know how to be around Josh. Although what had happened had been addressed back then, and he had apologized many times, we didn't talk about what had happened anymore. It felt like the distant past. But even so, I didn't expect him to be quite as relaxed as he was. And later in the days I didn't expect him to start laughing—even though it was clearly nervous laughter—when he described being under siege by photographers.

It felt weird that he was acting like this, but it was Mom who dealt with it.

"Josh," she barked. "It's not your fault that this was released, but you need to know that you were behind all this. Don't be so arrogant."

Josh's smile vanished. "I'm sorry," he said. "I'm sorry to you, girls, that y'all are having to go through all this."

Pops was in game plan mode. He and Chad spent most of the day huddling together, debating what the best next steps were and constantly taking calls. They'd share snatches of news, but it wasn't until the evening that we all finally got to sit around and listen to Pops explain everything to us.

He started by saying that TLC had paused the show and were considering canceling it altogether. It seemed painful for him to say it out loud, and he let the words hang in the air for the longest time. It was hard to see Pops like this. Hard to see him wounded. It was impossible for me to imagine what life would be like for him, Mom, and my younger siblings without the show in their lives. But the fight was not all gone from him.

"There are people out there who would like us to fade away. The world would like to see us close our doors and disappear. But we're not going to do that. We're not giving up on this ministry. The window of opportunity that God has opened for this family to show the world what it means to follow him is still there. They think we're damaged goods, but I will work with TLC to see what we can do to get this thing back up and going again."

Another pause. And then there was resolve in his voice once more. Pops was Pops again, rallying his troops.

"It was wrong what Josh did," he said, looking at us all. "But we will get past this. We will move on. We need to help TLC understand that this happened in the past, that this was something we have already dealt with."

In many ways he was right. This belonged in the past, and we had taken steps to deal with it. I had seen a professional counselor, per the court's recommendation during the DHS investigation, and my parents were always ready to listen if I wanted to talk. But by the time of the investigation, I didn't really want to talk about it, so it rarely came up. Maybe it would've been helpful for me to have had some earlier counseling when it first happened, and for sure it would have been helpful around the time all of this released in 2015, but unfortunately, like many people, I didn't know I needed it. So I buried it back in the past.

The conversation shifted to specifics, as Chad and Pops discussed the best way possible to change the narrative. Chad had connections with Fox News, so he talked about offering an exclusive interview to someone there.

"A world exclusive. The first interview. But who with?"

"No need for Josh to appear."

"No way. Maybe Michelle takes the lead?"

"That could work."

"Who does the interview? It's gotta be a female."

"Megyn Kelly?"

"Megyn would be great."

* * *

The more they talked, the worse I felt. I felt bad for my parents. Bad that they had to do all this. Bad that Pops' show was on the line here. Bad that the world wasn't able to see that my parents were good people just trying to do good things.

So even before they asked us girls how we felt about them doing an interview on TV, I knew what I was going to say. I knew that they needed someone to stand up for them, someone to vouch for them. They needed someone to do what they could to save the show.

I was one of the older kids, so I naturally felt more weight and responsibility to do something, to help somehow. And I wanted to help them, to show them my love and loyalty in this hardest of times. But I had no boundaries, no sense of what I needed to do to protect myself. I was terrified and didn't want to do the interview at all, but I felt like it was the only way to prove my love and commitment to my parents. I could clear their name and tell everyone that my brother's problems were a thing of the past. How could I stay silent?

I thought I knew how much it would cost me.

All that trauma I'd been feeling as I'd hidden behind the closed blinds at home, it was all going to get worse. That shame, that humiliation, those feelings of being victimized and violated all over again, they were all about to be magnified. Everything was about to get worse, but it was the cost that I had to pay.

"I would be willing," I said. "I'll do the interview."

A wave of nausea hit me, like nothing I'd ever experienced before. The room was spinning, the sound of blood rushing in my ear. I knew why I'd done it, but what had I done?

Then, without warning, a moment of hope.

"Me too," said Jessa. "I'll do it with you."

Pops looked at us both. "Are you sure?"

We nodded.

"Thank you," he said. "Thank you."

"Thank you," said another voice. I looked up. It was Josh.

The days that followed were chaotic. Chad wanted to go over the talking points with us, and Jessa and I talked a lot about how we could vouch for Mom and Pops. In a strange way I was grateful that there was no time to pause, no moment to think about what was coming or how I'd feel going on primetime TV to talk about the abuse. I was about to face the firing squad, and all I wanted to do was get it over with.

After the Megyn Kelly interview at the Big House. Ben, Jessa, Jim Bob, Michelle, Megyn, Jill, and Derick. June 2015.

———— ∞∞ ————

CHAPTER FIVE

Tearing Apart

"Do you still want to go?"

In the immediate aftermath of the release, Derick and I had not talked much about going to El Salvador. But it was getting close now. Decisions had to be made.

It had been less than two weeks since Jessa and I had sat down with Megyn Kelly. On that day we had taken our seats beneath the bright lights at the Big House and did what we could to stand up for our parents. Answering all Megyn's questions, with Josh watching from a couch just out of shot, was like having a bandage ripped off a deep and open wound. It was agony, so painful that I didn't really pause to ask why Josh was allowed to be there in the first place. What was worse was the fact that I'd hoped it would calm things down. It hadn't. The paparazzi were still chasing us, the internet still feasting on us, poring over every statement from the network, every new photo, every new angle. My nightmares were getting worse and there was nothing I could do to block any of it out. All I was doing was surviving from one breath to the next.

So yeah, I wanted to go. I felt like it was something we were called to do. But I knew there were risks. Being missionaries with this particular organization, we would be responsible for raising our own financial support. The show had given us a level of exposure that was way above anything we could have created for ourselves, but it had brought with it some complexities. We weren't naïve to the fact that we might be seen as some kind of target, so we chose not to reveal where we were going, and only ever talked about working in Central America. The last thing we wanted was for someone to be able to track us down.

The first thing that happened? Someone tracked us down. At least, that's what Derick and I were convinced had happened when we arrived in El Salvador and were told by Mike that he had just received a call from a Salvadorian journalist who wanted to come and write a piece about the mission.

Something about it didn't add up. The mission was small, and apart from Derick and I starting that month, there was nothing else new that had happened—certainly nothing that would cause a journalist to suddenly take interest and want to visit.

Mike didn't share our suspicions. He told us that he knew the journalist in question and had been interviewed by him in the past. All the same, I was glad when the baby and other demands kept me away from that area of the mission, out of the camera's eye on the day the journalist visited.

A few days later, when the *Sun* posted a grainy picture online of Derick at the mission, alongside a story about how we'd fled Arkansas and how they had tracked us down in El Salvador, Mike apologized. It was kind of him, but it was too late by then. The piece hadn't just named the country we were in, it even named the mission itself. The target on our back had just gotten a whole lot bigger and brighter.

To make matters worse, we soon discovered that there had been a recent increase in gang violence in the area. There were rumors of killings and kidnappings, and whispers that the wealthy were a particular target.

Despite the ever-present fear of what might happen if we got caught up in the gang violence, life in El Salvador had its good parts. We stayed on the mission's property while a mission multipurpose house was being built overlooking a valley that was densely packed with banana trees and a whole bunch of other jungle plants I didn't recognize. I divided my days between caring for Israel and running groups with local women and girls. We had no AC, no Wi-Fi, intermittent electricity, and an army of fire ants that were desperate to take over the kitchen. It took some adjusting to, but growing up in a large family I had learned to be patient and not always have everything I ever wanted. Thanks to the show, we'd lived well for years, but I didn't miss the luxuries. It felt good to figure out how to do laundry without all the usual appliances, and how to clean food while being careful about the contaminated water.

Arkansas and being part of a filming family felt just a little further away, and I was grateful for a little more space. The show still had a hold on us, and a lot of time was taken up with emails, conversations, and a lot of filming on our own. But the location and the rhythm of life made it easier to cope with the filming requirements that had remained with us, for which we had to make the occasional

Jill, Derick, and baby Israel, June 2015

trip back home. Whenever we could, we savored the moments of calm that this simple life brought us.

I was grateful, too, for the opportunity to see Derick in mission mode once again. He thrived on the work, and I was sure that I'd never seen him so peaceful or so content as when he was sitting on the back balcony, looking out over the valley with his Bible open on his lap and his notebook ready beside him.

Derick didn't look so peaceful or content the day he connected to Wi-Fi and logged into Twitter.

"Hey babe. I just read something about Josh," he said. "People are saying that he's been caught logging in to some website called

Ashley Madison, for people who want to have extramarital affairs. I googled it, and there are a bunch of tabloids running the story."

I felt my heart plunge in my chest.

But I decided to play it differently this time, to be active instead of passively waiting for the story to emerge. I wanted to know the truth, so instead of ignoring it or waiting for my parents to tell me what was going on, or trying to get information through the grapevine from my siblings, Derick and I decided that it would be best if I texted Josh right away. I wanted to hear directly from him, to know whether there was any truth in the rumors.

In El Salvador, 2015

I got no reply.

A day or two later, Mom called. "It's been devastating for Anna and the kids," she said, and I could hear the same weary, frustrated tone that she had used in the Oklahoma cabin just a couple of months earlier. She told me that the rumors were true, that Josh had confessed that he'd been addicted to pornography for years, and that he had paid to join a social networking site for people wanting to cheat on their spouses.

By the time the call ended, I felt just as weary and just as mad at Josh and the whole situation as Mom.

This time, it was up to me to share the news with Derick.

"What happens now?" he asked.

"He is being sent away," I sighed. "Again."

We had agreed to work with Mike's mission in El Salvador for two years but had some prior commitments—mainly involving my midwifery training—back in the US that meant we had to return home briefly. So, not too long after Josh's affair news broke, we flew back to Arkansas and made our way back to Tontitown.

It was fall, a season filled with so many great memories of home—trips to Silver Dollar City, our favorite theme park, and long games of Bible charades at home, where one older sibling would lead three or more little ones in re-creating anything from David and Goliath to the stoning of Stephen. We had so much fun back then, but when we returned from El Salvador, the Big House felt different to me. There was no Scott, no TV cameras, no visitors sitting with Pops in his office, the Big House had lost its usual buzz of excitement. It felt somber. Mom looked tired. A lot of my siblings looked stressed. But that evening when we joined the greater Duggar family for Bible time in the living room, Pops had some news to share.

"Hey guys," he said after we'd greeted each other, hugged, and everyone had made a fuss over Israel. "I just talked to Josh and the guy who runs the place where he is staying. He seems to be doing good. He's been working in the kitchen. And the guy who runs the program says he's doing really well. He said he's been like a role model for some of the others and that he's their best person there."

Mom had told me about the program—a Christian-run rehab center up in Rockford, Illinois. I knew nothing about rehab, but it sounded better than sending him away to work construction.

"We had some trouble getting him up there," said Pops. "The paparazzi were trying real hard to find out where he was going. They even tracked the tail number of his flight. But at least we got him in there without him being seen. The guy who runs the program said they had some photographers show up at the open chapel looking for Josh. But the staff there have been very kind to us and they were able to find a way to keep him out of sight. I just wanted to update everyone, as we are happy to receive a good report and we pray that God continues to work in his life while he is there."

The conversation changed soon after that, but I was left with his words ringing in my head like a bell. Though I love my parents and it made a lot of sense that they would want to protect and care for their child, I couldn't help but think about the lengths that Pops had gone to in order to guard Josh's privacy and keep him from being publicly humiliated. I mentioned this to Derick, and he said that he had noticed the same thing. The feelings grew stronger within me, and by the time I went to bed I felt sick to my core.

When the *In Touch* story broke, all I had wanted was to be protected. All I'd wanted was to have privacy and space to grieve without feeling the weight upon myself to fix the situation. I knew that in time we were all going to do what we could to fight for justice in the legal system that had failed us, initiating a lawsuit against the magazine and the people who were behind the illegal release of the records. I also knew my dad would fight hard too, and I was so grateful for that support. But back when we'd sat in that cabin discussing the show, what I'd really wanted was for Pops to say, "No, we're not going to put you on Fox News. I'm going to do everything I can to keep you girls out of this. We are not concerned about the future of our show anymore." I wanted my daddy to stand up for me in that way. Had he known that? Would he have done something different if I'd spoken up? I had no idea. I'd spent much of my life listening to IBLP teaching on the "umbrella of protection." When I'd needed it most, it had failed me. It felt as though I, as a woman, was expected do all I could to protect Pops and Josh. Nobody appeared to see it differently.

We were back in the US for a few weeks, and during our stay there we spent plenty of time over at the Big House. It was good to be with the family, especially without the presence of TV crews for just a few weeks before things picked back up full force. Though our show and all the reruns had been pulled from their regular airtime back when everything was released in May 2015, filming hadn't taken much of a break for long. My mom, Jessa, and I had already shot one scene for the network in August in NYC, and there was talk of more show plans picking back up soon. In between studying for my upcoming exam, we were very busy catching up on doctor visits as well as continuing to raise support and meet with people to update them on our ministry. For a while at least, it almost felt like a normal family.

But . . . normal families don't have family meetings where execs from a TV network roll up and pitch the idea of starting a new show. That's what happened one day in mid-September when we were back home. Pops introduced the network guys, and I recognized the girl who spoke first. I'd seen her at various media appearances, and most recently the Megyn Kelly interview. She might even have been at my wedding. I wasn't sure. With a guest list of two thousand, it was impossible to keep track of who had and hadn't been there.

"We don't want to punish the victims," she said, looking around. "So we've been trying to figure out how to get the show back up and running. At the beginning, we're going to focus only on the older kids who are adults, but especially those who are married and have moved out of the house. Eventually we might be able to come back around to showing the younger kids and your parents, but Josh will not be on the show. We cannot have him part of it at all."

I could feel the whole room shifting its focus onto Josh's wife, Anna. She sat silent and still, like a rabbit hoping a hunter would just move on.

"Before we continue," said the network representative, "we want to make sure that you guys are on board."

Our producer, Scott, spoke up. "We'll have to rebrand the show, give it a new name and a whole new filming style—no more cutting back to old footage like before. It's all fresh, all new." He paused and looked at us older kids. "We can't bring the show back without you. What do you say?"

In spite of everything I'd just heard, it felt a little like a watered-down rerun of the Oklahoma cabin conversation to me. I wanted to be helpful to Pops, I wanted to show him that I was on his side, but what about the cost? I wasn't sure that either Derick or I saw there being a whole lot of room for the show in our future. The mission field was where our hearts belonged.

My siblings were taking it in turns to voice their support and agree to the new show. When it was time for Derick and me to speak, he said that life was complicated for us now that we were in El Salvador. "It's dangerous down there," he added. "If we draw too much attention to ourselves or the mission, it could cause problems." We wanted to help, but made it clear that our involvement would likely look different now. We would be gone again soon, and this time when we returned to Central America, per our commitment, we would not be coming back to the States at all for several months. If they were going to have us on the show, they'd have to be flexible and creative, especially as they were thinking of calling it *Jill and Jessa: Counting On*. We wanted them to know for sure that Derick and I were firmly committed to pursuing our calling as missionaries. The rep listened, then talked about us having approval over all content. Derick and I exchanged glances, and I knew that, like me, he thought it could work.

When we had all agreed, the rep had one final point to raise.

"If we're going to do the show again, we can't just skip over what happened. Anna's going to have to sit down and talk about the affair, and the rest of you are going to have to talk about what happened with the magazine. Are you going to be okay with that?"

We all froze. I don't think any of us were okay with it, but the play had already been set with the Megyn Kelly interview. Going on TV, opening our most painful wounds for the sake of the ratings, it was what it looked like when you were a TV family.

I felt for Anna. She'd been through so much already. And now it was going to get worse.

Even though we'd agreed to the trip back to the US before we took up our post in El Salvador, spending six weeks in the US so soon after we'd begun our work at the mission wasn't ideal. When we returned to El Salvador in December, Mike asked that we commit to remaining there until the following July. No more trips back to the US. We gladly agreed. We wanted to be all in, all the time.

Things felt different when we returned. It wasn't just the twenty-two hundred miles between us and Arkansas, or the fact that communication was so difficult. The new show marked a new beginning, and we had made some fundamental changes to the way we interacted with those running it. Earlier in the year, around the time we were leaving for Central America, we had set up a 501c3 and asked Chad to help us with our fundraising. In the fall, when we headed back and filming had picked back up, we also decided to ask him to be our main point of contact for the network. Suddenly it didn't feel like Pops was the one asking us about when we could film or what we could commit to, and we'd hoped it would help the show become more balanced and feel like less of a burden. With Chad on our side, we hoped that we might be able to avoid some of the emotion when it came to negotiating our involvement with the show. For a while at least, I felt optimistic. Maybe the commitment would be managable and the show would give Derick and I just enough exposure to continue raising the funds we needed to remain on the mission field.

There was one more reason things felt different. In the short time we had been away, the gang situation in El Salvador had gotten even worse. There were a lot more police on patrol in the capital, San Salvador, and in our little village some of the shops and houses had started hiring armed guards. We'd had our own guard ever since we'd arrived, but it didn't feel like much protection anymore.

One evening, while Derick was off somewhere, I was with a few of the ladies on the team inside our room in the church. It was quiet and remote where we lived, so we all heard the single gunshot that echoed across the valley. We froze. It was close. When the second shot rang out soon after, we panicked. Two of the older moms hurried me into a closet, and as I squatted on the floor—with Israel pressed close to me—I listened to the sounds of feet scurrying around as the others found places to hide.

Minutes passed. It was hot in the closet. The air was stale and lifeless. I listened hard, but there was no sound coming from the other side of the closet doors. I had no idea whether that was a good sign or not.

My heart was screaming in my chest, the sound of blood in my ears almost deafening. I wanted to call out and see what was going on, but if this was a possible kidnapping, our survival depended on us going undetected.

Israel started to squirm to let me know that he was hot too. He took a breath and made the noise that he always made before he started to cry. I fed him, desperately hoping that it would work.

After about ten minutes, someone gave the all clear. One of the guards at the other end of the property had been showing off and had let a friend fire his gun.

At first I was relieved. Then I was annoyed that the whole thing had been caused by someone acting so foolishly. As the sky grew dark, I was worried. That night, for once, my nightmares weren't set in a dark Arkansas bedroom.

Most of the time gunfire was a rarity, and life started to find its rhythm. Each week brought with it a rich array of opportunities to pray with people, for Derick to preach, for us to visit a local orphanage, and to generally spend quality time being a mom of a little one alongside other moms and their babies. My family had been visiting the mission down there for years, and I was glad that many of the people we were working among considered themselves our friends. In the strangest of ways, I felt at home down there.

As Christmas approached, it was time for the annual mission trip to El Salvador. As usual, a handful of Duggars were coming, including Pops and several of my siblings—as well as a new friend of theirs, a great guy named Jeremy, who my sister, Jinger, was getting to know.

Six months had passed since we had formed Dillard Family Ministries, our 501c3. We'd posted about it on our family blog, and so many people had been generous in response. That initial burst of financial support was amazing, but since moving, the fundraising had gotten a lot harder. Money was flowing out of our ministry bank account a lot faster than it was coming in. Like any other missionary family, we discovered quickly that fundraising when you're on the field is hard work. Things were a little more complicated for us because of being on TV—and we'd had a few comments from people on Twitter, who assumed that we were making a lot of money off the show and shouldn't need to go asking people for help. Derick wanted to set them straight, explaining that we didn't make a dime off the show, and that our involvement in it was purely voluntary, but per my request, he stayed quiet. We figured that if we could do a good job of presenting what we were doing, and Chad could help us with providing updates and maybe putting on church events and meet and greets when we came back to the US, then that fundraising might just get a little easier.

The mission house that Mike's ministry had been building was completed just in time for us to move in during the first week of December, just before the Christmas mission team arrived. Mike was excited to show us the place, and a couple days later when Pops and some of my siblings arrived with the rest of the team, we showed them around too. The house was pretty empty, so Mike took Pops and a few other people to the city one day to shop for some household items. They came back with a washing machine, a rice cooker, and a few other things. For a mama with a little one in reusable diapers, that was a good day.

*   *   *

A few nights into the trip, Pops, Derick, and I were sitting around our dimly lit bedroom as I nursed Israel to sleep. It was a typical night on the edge of the jungle, and all of us were feeling wiped out by the ninety-degree heat and 100 percent humidity. Our single fan was no match for the conditions.

I don't remember who brought it up, but somehow we started talking about the show, the filming schedule, and our availability. Suddenly, without warning, the topic shifted onto a subject that I had always avoided discussing with my parents. Money.

With his background in accounting, Derick always paid special attention to our finances, and he was starting to get concerned when looking to the future that the initial fundraising was not sustainable. As we continued to talk about ministry fundraising efforts and keeping supporters in the loop via regular ministry email and blog updates, we were also reminded, on a different note, about our personal finances.

Even though our ministry finances were completely separate from our personal finances, it spurred our thinking. Since the start of the new, rebranded show—*Jill and Jessa: Counting On*—we couldn't help but think again about when we might see some income for all of our previous and current involvement.

After arriving back in El Salvador, Derick and I had talked a few times about the fact that we had never seen any income for our work on the show, but I would always feel bad about going there, so I'd circle back to remind him about the show being a ministry, which is where the conversations always ended.

But tonight, with Pops in the room, Derick wanted to talk.

"I'm just wondering, Pops, do you think we could maybe see some kind of income from the show at some point?"

Pops tensed. I cringed, bracing for impact. He looked genuinely shocked. When he regained his composure, his words were carefully measured.

"Derick, from the very beginning, our family has viewed this as a ministry. An opportunity to share with the world that children are a blessing. Back when we started this show, we didn't make anything off it. I was the one who was able to negotiate a good deal for our family. I could retire right now. The only reason I'm still doing this is for you kids."

Pops sat back. Question dodged. Conversation over.

I looked at Derick. I could tell he was thinking. It was like he was checking a column of calculations a second and third time before hitting return. Eventually, he spoke again.

"Well, how about us receiving a certain percentage of what comes in? Could that work?"

Pops paused, his jaw set tight. "We used to pay Josh, but decided not to do that after a while because it wasn't a very good idea." Then he shifted, smiling at us both and changing course, seemingly looking for another way to shut things down. "Michelle is the one that has had all these kids. We wouldn't even have this show if it weren't for her."

It was obvious that Pops wanted us to pick up on his cues and bow out of this dance, but Derick wasn't giving in. He was respectful, but his voice was firm and his demeanor unwavering. "Yes, that's true, but we've also added a lot of value to the show and done a lot to contribute. After all, the show is called *Jill and Jessa: Counting On*."

It was a game of chess. I knew there were other moves Derick could make, like mentioning the fact that our wedding alone had drawn 4.4 million viewers for hours of prime-time television, or that as a couple we'd taken part in multiple *People* magazine cover shoots to promote both the wedding and Israel's birth episodes, which had been big successes themselves.

Pops was quick to respond. "I know y'all did some iPhone video or something for the pregnancy and birth stuff, and we appreciate all of that, but it takes teamwork. We all have to help out. Like some of the kids are filming a lot in other areas of their lives. And at times some will be more involved than others, but it averages out in the long run."

For a moment I thought Pops was done with the conversation. But he surprised me.

Turning to Derick he asked, "What are you worth? Ten dollars an hour? Twelve? That's what I pay some of the others who work for me."

It was the first I'd ever heard of Pops paying anyone in the family, but I could read the signs. It wasn't an invitation to debate or discuss, and it certainly wasn't a joke. It was a dismissal. He wanted us to back off, to go into full retreat. But Derick wasn't having any of it.

"Well," said Derick, remaining calm, "what's the show worth?"

"Huh?"

"You can't appraise the value of a worker to a business until you know what the whole business is worth. So I guess before we can tell you what we're worth, we'd need to know what kind of deal you've got with TLC."

Pops' mood soured further. He was already upset, and the effort to stay calm was starting to show. "Derick, when we got into this, all those years ago, we just really wanted to reach people to show that children are a blessing. It's not something we went looking for. God brought this opportunity to us, and we really feel like he has blessed it and helped us reach so many people, many who would otherwise never step foot in a church. Nearly every day we are getting emails from people who say they've been impacted. They've shared how they've given their lives to Jesus, or started going to church again, or decided to have more children, just by seeing Christian values portrayed through the show. Think about how many people we've been able to reach on a secular television network. I'm not saying your work here isn't great, but we are reaching more people through the show than you are here on the mission field."

The sting was sharp.

All the while Pops and Derick had been talking, I'd been cringing, trying to hide myself away right there on the bed, wishing that the conversation would stop. All my internal alarms about pushing back on authority had been going off full volume. But Pops' comment had bite. It hurt. It felt like it was designed to make us back off.

But Derick didn't scare so easily.

"I understand, Pops. But we would be so grateful if you could pray about maybe possibly paying us something. Jill has contributed a lot of hours to filming over the past decade, and she has nothing to show for it financially. I know she's the first daughter to get married and that you are still figuring this out, so we get that it's awkward, but I'm sure as more of the other kids get older and marry too, they'll be thinking of these things also."

When Pops left our room, Derick and I talked a little longer, prayed, then went to bed. Derick had no trouble sleeping, but I was wired too tight. I was anxious and panicking, and my heart was threatening to burst its way out of my chest. I wasn't used to seeing someone talk back and press Pops like that. I was worried that we would be seen as disrespectful, even though Derick had been polite throughout. In the culture I had been raised in, questioning a parent's authority was a very negative thing, and I hated the thought of rocking the boat like that. Nobody had ever done it before, but I was sure that if anyone did, the punishment would be severe, most likely resulting in effective banishment from the family. But I was also with Derick on wanting more information about the finances of filming. So, long into the night, I stared into the darkness, hoping and praying that we could work things out with Pops soon and get more information without causing any problems.

Somewhere in the middle of those long, humid hours, with the cicadas making their constant chorus outside, my thoughts turned to Derick. He wasn't plagued by guilt or bound by fear. It reminded me of what Jesus said in the Bible about children not being afraid to ask their father for bread.

I felt something change inside me. I was still mortified by the thought of Pops feeling angry with us. But I was proud of my husband too. He'd fought for his family, just like he'd promised to do on the day we got married.

The rest of the mission trip passed without incident between Pops and us. We spent good times with several of my siblings who were old enough to come on the trip, and we hoped that Pops would do what we'd asked and pray about starting to pay us and some of the other kids.

Almost as soon as they left, the security situation in the area got worse. We heard rumors of increased gang activity, and we were warned that even walking for a minute or two on our own in the wrong street would put us at risk for kidnapping. We tried not to give too much oxygen to the fear, but we felt like we had a target on our backs, and it felt like our worries were further affirmed with the news that TLC had decided to take out ransom insurance on us, which only made us feel even more vulnerable. No matter how much we wanted to blend in and be part of the community, we knew we stood out. We were the only white people in the area. When we'd visited when I was a kid, it had never bothered me at all, but now, with the dangers increasing, and me as a wife and mama having so much more to lose, it felt different. People encouraged us to keep an unpredictable schedule as much as possible, but that was hard to do while trying to be consistent in ministry.

In the end, it wasn't us they came for.

Pretty much every male in the country was in a gang, even boys as young as seven and eight. There were only two ways of getting out—you either died, or you joined a church. For some reason, the gangs left Christians alone, but only if the person was genuinely committed to their church. Even then, the gangs still forced those non-members to pay taxes or "rent" for their freedom.

We had been attending and helping in various ministries at the local church affiliated with the ministry we were working with ever since we arrived, and we were starting to become good friends with the people there, especially with one family who lived ten minutes from our house. One of their daughters, Fatima, had a boyfriend who had gotten out of a gang. Raul was sixteen or seventeen, and we'd see him at church from time to time.

One day while Raul was out in the street, a car pulled up and took him. Nobody ever saw or heard from him again. Everybody assumed the same two things—that someone, somewhere, had noticed that he hadn't been a regular at church, and that Raul was now dead. Not long after, Fatima and her mother, Rosa, showed up at the church in tears. They told us that the gang had instructed them not to ask any questions or look for Raul or his body, and that if they did, they would be next.

As the violence continued, we decided to get a permanent guard of our own, not just for when the mission's teams were with us. It was yet another expense that we couldn't afford, but the risk of not having someone armed to protect us was just too great.

We didn't have a television in El Salvador, and even if we had, the shows usually aired later internationally, so we weren't keeping up with the show and for a while felt like it was happening on a different planet. That didn't last long. As soon as season one of *Jill and Jessa: Counting On* aired just before Christmas, there was an increase in emails and phone calls as TLC made plans for season two. We were given instructions to shoot a lot of content ourselves—home video of anything from us eating a meal, to Israel starting to walk—and since the arrangement was more conducive to our schedule, it worked out okay.

The request that Chad emailed to us after Christmas was a whole other matter. TLC wanted to shoot some new promotional content for commercials, and they wanted all of us adult Duggar children involved in the show to fly to Houston for a few days in February.

Even though the show was technically about us adult children and had been branded to look different from the old *19 Kids and Counting*, everything behind the scenes was the same. Scott was still the producer, Pops was still the only one being paid and the one in control of the contract, and Chad was still the one carrying out Pops' and the network's bidding, making sure everyone stayed in line and behaved as they were supposed to in order to get this new series off the ground.

Back in October, when we'd left Arkansas and returned to El Salvador, we'd told Chad and everybody else about the commitment we'd made to Mike to stay in the country until the end of July 2016. When Chad asked us about going to Houston for filming, we figured that maybe Chad had forgotten this, so we apologized that we couldn't make it and reminded him that we had given our word that we would remain in El Salvador.

He didn't reply, but in January Chad did email us to say that since he was about to book tickets to Houston, we needed to tell him which flight we wanted.

We wrote back, telling Chad that we were not going to be able to make it, reminding him again of our deal with Mike.

Chad's email back was polite but insistent. He explained that the shoot was vital for the promotion that the network was planning for the show, and that our presence was key. "It is a big deal for them," he wrote. "They've offered if you have a list of things you need from the States that you cannot get in CA, they will do that shopping for you and pack those things up to go back with you."

We got back to him quickly, repeating our commitment to Mike. But we did say that we would pray about it more and let him know that we would be talking with Pops and Mom later that evening.

The next day, after talking with my parents and praying, we slept on it. Our parents had been supportive, though clear that they wanted us to figure something out with Chad, and even more clear that they thought the shoot was important. We went back to Chad the next day and told him that we felt that our time in the field was important and that we needed to honor our commitment, so traveling back wasn't an option. We suggested that we could shoot some video and send it on to them, or they could have the crew fly down and meet us at a San Salvador airport hotel and do the shoot in front of a green screen in an afternoon. We hoped that somehow we could figure out a compromise.

We couldn't.

Eventually, after several emails, Derick picked up the phone and called Chad. "We don't have to come back," he said. "Jill isn't obligated to anything. Jill and I have only ever been volunteers."

Chad shot back, "Jill has a contractual obligation. She has to return."

"Excuse me? Jill has never signed any contract."

The call ended soon after and was followed by an email from Chad outlining what he alleged I was obligated to—a pasted list of various obligations toward the show, including that we would make ourselves available to all promotional activities as requested by the network. Chad's email referenced a contract that I signed, and that the contract was fixed for five years.

I was confused.

Derick was suspicious. "Do you remember ever being part of any contract deals with the network?"

"No," I said. "Never. Pops always handled all communication with the network."

I was upset, confused, and immensely disturbed by the idea of there being some kind of actual contract out there that might obligate me to things beyond my control—a contract of which I had zero recollection of ever signing.

As the weeks passed, while I was stressing about this phantom contract, the attempts to get us to agree to go to Houston increased. The phone calls and pressure continued to build, but we heard less from Chad and more from my parents. We asked Chad and Pops to send us a copy of whatever contract we were obligated to, but still nobody would give us anything. They just kept pressuring us about the shoot, repeating that I was obligated to attend.

The more they pressed, the more we pushed back. The only commitment I felt obligated to was the one we had made to Mike to serve the mission fully.

Three days out from the shoot, the phone rang. It was early morning, and even before I looked at the screen, I knew who would be calling. Pops had called twice already that day.

Saying no to the Houston trip felt like torture, but Derick and I had been doing it for weeks now, and we were committed to standing firm. After years and years of compromise and giving in to whatever demands the network made, finally we had found a hill to die on. This was our moment to take a stand. We were not doing it to make things difficult for the network or for Pops. We wanted to make everyone happy. We wanted to work things out and we were still trying to be as accommodating as possible. However, we just felt like we had to make the right choice. Instead of feeling happy or empowered, I felt angry that things had come to this. Angry, and terrified too.

"Pops . . . ," I said, trying to get a word in as soon as he began. "That's not . . . that's not what we're saying . . ."

The tension made my voice sound different. Younger, like I was twelve instead of twenty-five. Maybe that's what he wanted, to put the right kind of pressure on the right nerves. But I didn't want to cave and just give in. I wanted Pops to understand why we were taking a stand like this. I wanted him to know that we'd made a commitment to *our* ministry. I wanted him to be proud of us for that, but instead all I could hear in his voice was frustration.

"It's so important that you're there for this. It's *Jill and Jessa: Counting On*, and they need you. Surely Mike can spare you for one day?"

Derick came and stood beside me, his arm around my shoulders. My heart was racing. I felt sick.

I put Pops on speakerphone so we both could hear what he was saying, but his request hadn't changed in any of the calls he'd made over the previous days. He wanted us on a plane that weekend, arriving in Houston in time for the shoot. But while the request was the same, his tone was different. On all the other calls he'd tried to persuade us. Now he was trying to guilt us.

"Is this you or is this Derick who is being the problem here?"

I'd never heard Pops say something like that before, and it pierced like a dagger to hear him try to pit us against each other like that. I was speechless.

"This isn't like you, Sweet Jilly Muffin. Is Derick behind this? Are you having problems financially? Are you depressed?"

I could feel Derick tensing beside me.

"Pops," he said, his voice calm and controlled. "We really aren't trying to ruin anything. We wish we could help, but we've made a commitment here."

There was pause before Pops spoke. When he did, his voice had a new, harsher edge to it.

"If you don't come back for this filming thing, everything's going to get messed up. We just got the show back up and going again, and we need to be real careful not to rock the boat with the network. They can't film the promotional material for *Jill and Jessa: Counting On* without you, Jill. Just think about it, if you don't come to this shoot and TLC cancels the show again, everyone is going to look at you and know that it's your fault and that you could have stopped it. Are you gonna be okay carrying that burden?"

"Hey . . . ," Derick said, stepping in to defend me.

"Let me talk to you for a minute, Derick, because you are causing your wife to go against her word. Is that what you're going to do? Make her break her word? If so, let me tell you that you are failing your family and leading them down a path of destruction. Are you prepared for that? Do you know what happens if you break a legally binding contract?"

It was the first time he'd mentioned the contract other than in email, though we still hadn't seen it. I could feel the blood rush to my face. I was so angry.

There was a moment's silence.

"You know," said Pops, "maybe you should flip a coin."

"Excuse me?" said Derick.

"A coin. I did it when I was trying to decide whether to run for US Senate. I flipped it three times and it came up heads every time. That's how I knew I should run."

Both of us sat in silence. That only seemed to make Pops more upset.

"Let me tell you something now! You're gonna get sued! You're gonna need whatever money you have, because you're going to be sued!"

Pops called back later that same day. And for the first time, we didn't answer. We just let the phone ring.

We did the same thing with the next call too.

And the next.

I felt a glimmer of relief, but it was more than overshadowed by the strong sense of guilt that we were disrespecting him this way.

My head was spinning, my stomach clamped painfully tight. Even on silent, the sound of the phone buzzing into life felt like the gunshots that had sent us into hiding months earlier. I felt tense and anxious. There was no closet deep or dark enough for me to hide in this time.

Finally, we turned off our phones.

My anxiety only got worse.

All afternoon I was in agony, flipping between fear and guilt every few seconds. I felt like I was in labor, but not like I'd been with Israel. This was no new life that I was bringing into the world, and there was no sense that if we could just get through this storm with Pops then everything would be okay. On the contrary, I was terrified that things were about to get a whole lot worse.

Later, when it was dark and all we could hear from outside were the sounds of the cicadas, I finally began to cry. Derick was holding me close, trying to make me feel safe and protected. But all I could feel was fear and guilt. Guilt and fear. My own father didn't recognize me. Didn't like me. Maybe he didn't even love me anymore.

What had I done?

What had I become?

"What if he's right, Derick?" I sobbed in the darkness. "What if we show up in America and we're taken to jail?"

Derick held me tighter, telling me everything was going to be fine.

"They're not going to sue the poor missionaries in Central America who have no contractual obligation and who haven't received so much as a cent in return for their work."

But the fear I felt was so real. I was convinced that by disrespecting Pops like this, by stepping out from under the umbrella of his protection, I was placing myself in great danger. If the courts didn't punish me, maybe God would.

On the day of the shoot, when my adult siblings were in Houston, I woke up feeling different. Not totally better, but not as bad as before. Some of the guilt had eased, and the fear wasn't quite so tight around my throat anymore. I felt like I could breathe again. We'd made it all the way to Saturday, and we hadn't given in. For the first time in my life, it felt like I was standing up for myself.

Saturdays were always busy in El Salvador, and this one was no different. We always worked in a local village that had a lot of gang activity, coordinating job skills training and teaching a Bible study. Besides that, Derick had a Sunday sermon to finish preparing for. It was good to feel like we were doing something, good to be distracted.

I was just finishing feeding Israel when I heard a vehicle approach out front. Then car doors slammed shut, and a voice I'd recognize anywhere called out.

"Hey! Derick? Jill? Are you there?"

I opened the door and saw them, Mom and Pops, coming down the stairs. Her eyes were kind of teary. Pops was behind his phone, filming this family reunion.

I didn't know what to say. My Sweet Jilly Muffin mask wasn't appearing on command. Derick was stunned too.

"We wanted to come and see you," said Pops after an awkward pause. "Didn't we, Michelle?"

She nodded and Pops put the phone away. He looked right at me. I could feel the walls edge closer, and I braced for impact.

"I realize I was a little harsh," he said. "I'm sorry for some of the things I said."

I reached for Derick's hand. If ever I needed to be reminded that my husband and I were united, it was then.

—∞—

CHAPTER SIX

No Agreement

The first week of August 2016, we boarded the plane for northwest Arkansas. There was a lot to be thankful for, and a lot to think about. Derick and I were both glad that we had been able to honor our promise to Mike, and we both were feeling like we had left behind good friends and a thriving ministry. It had been hard to say good-bye, even though we were only planning on being back in the US for two to three months. We were due to attend two weddings—one for Derick's brother, the other for my sister Jinger—and do a ton of filming required for the show. The weddings I was super excited about. The filming, not so much. There were extensive plans for the crew to follow us as we all prepared for the wedding, plus capture a ton of everyday activities, like going to the grocery store, so that we could talk about all the things we'd missed while we'd been away.

That final flight on the long journey home was anything but settled. Israel was just a year old and didn't want to sit still for more than a few minutes at a time. Inside, I felt just as restless. Just as unsettled. The closer we got to home, the worse I felt.

A few months earlier we'd finally received a partial copy of the infamous contract that Chad had mentioned. Not the whole contract, but a few excerpts—including a clause that stated I had to reveal to the network if I discovered I was pregnant, as well as the final page that had mine and my siblings' signatures inked in.

That signature page was instantly familiar, especially when I read the date that I'd signed it.

June 20, 2014.

The day before Derick and I were married. The day Pops had told me that he had some simple papers for us all to sign in the dining room, saying that it only had to do with how we were going to get paid—not that we'd ever received any wages for any of our work.

I'd been furious when I'd found out, but now that we were heading back to see the family for the first time, I was calmer. But I was still nervous.

The whole family was waiting for us. So was a film crew, which left me wondering just how honest the hugs and the "welcome backs" and the "we love yous" really were.

It turned out they were genuine. Once the cameras left and we were back at the Big House, it was like the whole Houston shoot conflict had never happened. I even began to think—to hope—that Pops' apology when he and Mom had showed up that day was completely genuine. We hadn't spoken much since then. Maybe he'd come around to our way of thinking and would be willing to talk about paying us fairly for our work. Maybe he saw the true value of what we were doing in El Salvador and wouldn't have to lessen its importance in comparison to the show all the time.

And so, with every conversation, every shared meal, every moment that I braced for impact and didn't get chewed out by Pops, I could feel myself relaxing. There were still a ton of questions floating around in my mind about the contract and why Pops had tricked me into signing it, and I still felt uneasy about the way he'd tried to drive a wedge between Derick and me on that phone call. But I was okay with leaving those for another day. We were going to enjoy the short time we had planned to spend at home, then return to the mission field ready for another period of service.

It didn't take long for that settled peace to change. But the disruption wasn't anything to do with Pops or the show. It wasn't even a bad thing. What threw our plans into the air was all down to me and Derick. I got pregnant again.

In any other year, nothing would have changed. Derick and I would have happily moved back to El Salvador just a few weeks later, confident that the little one would grow just as well in my womb down in Central America as it would back in the States. But 2016 wasn't any other year. The Zika virus was raging across Latin America, and it posed an even higher risk to women in their early stages of pregnancy.

Ultimately, due to filming demands, including a promotional shoot in December we were required to attend, we had to wait until at least the end of the year to return to El Salvador. Mike was gracious and said he understood, and we agreed that we'd return soon after the shoot. Besides keeping Dillard baby number two healthy, it allowed us to be fully available for whatever the show required. Even though mine and Jessa's names were in the title, the show actually divided its focus among several of us older kids. Jana, John-David, Joseph, Josiah, Joy, and Anna were all featured in addition to us, and with Jinger engaged to Jeremy, and another wedding on the horizon, we weren't as much of a focus as we had been in the first few seasons of *Counting On*. After thirteen years of filming—almost half my life—I was finally starting to imagine a future without it.

Derick and I enjoyed having time and space to talk and dream and pray about what our lives might look like once we'd completed the second year in El Salvador. We'd loved being part of the mission project, but our time was coming to an end. At the same time our baby was growing secretly inside me, we were also starting to nurture plans for what we might do next in our lives.

Family meeting. 10 am tomorrow morning.

Pops' text came through early one October morning, to a group made up of the older kids. Pops was always sending messages to different ones of us—those who lived at the Big House, those who were older, those who were younger (but not the smallest kids), married kids, single kids—but there was something triggering about being called to a family meeting. The wounds from the last few that I'd attended were still raw.

When Pops started by talking about Josh, it all sounded so familiar.

"He's had a few more struggles," Pops said once everyone had sat down and the door was closed. "Y'all already know that Josh has recently got his own car lot, and so we feel like it's best for him to go out on his own now."

Pops stopped. His words were typically vague, designed to shut debate down, not invite it. So while there were a ton of questions that we could have asked, nobody said anything. Our main job in these family meetings was usually just to listen. Substantive issues were not up for discussion.

But it turned out that the meeting wasn't about Josh after all.

"Anyway," Pops said, smiling, "Mom and I have been talking, and some of the boys are getting older and are to the point where they could use some money to help move on in life. And we thought it might be a good idea for you guys to have a little bit of money so that y'all can do what you need to do in life. We want to give you each eighty thousand dollars, and I'm guessing some of you will use it to start your businesses, buy houses, or whatever to get yourselves started."

The room burst into a chorus of surprise and gratitude. In all my life, I'd hardly ever been more surprised by something that Pops said.

"You know," he continued once the room was quieter, "you guys can thank Derick for this. He's been talking to me about paying some of you guys."

To everybody else, the comment was a throw away. But to Derick and me, sitting side by side, it was a trigger. I was glad Pops had finally decided to pay something outright to some of the kids, and glad too that he recognized Derick for his involvement in the process, but my mind took me back to the humid bedroom that we'd sat in with Pops before Christmas, Derick looking confused and exasperated. Pops looking mad. Me feeling like I was in a whole world of trouble. Bracing for impact as the plane hurtled toward earth.

I swallowed my feelings and reached for my husband's hand. I gave him three squeezes, received four in return, and waited to see if Pops was going to say anything else about Derick and me.

He didn't.

"All I'm going to need is for y'all to sign something. I'm having the paperwork drawn up now. Once you've signed, I'll get you the money."

As soon as we were alone, Derick said exactly what I was thinking.

"I don't get it. It raises so many questions. Why eighty thousand? Why now?"

"And what's it for? Is this us getting paid for the shows we've already done, or is it a gift?"

We talked late into the night but got nowhere. We felt frustrated to be left with so many questions and only Pops to answer them. And based on recent history, we didn't feel comfortable taking all our questions to him anyway. A discussion might just leave us with no real information again, and more heartache. Maybe Pops was just being generous, but both of us felt sure that there was some angle he was playing. After all, thirteen years as a filming family had taught that everything has a cost. Plus, Pops' lifestyle alone told us that the show had generated a lot more than the equivalent of eighty thousand dollars each.

At first, the changes had been subtle. We'd enjoyed more extravagant presents at Christmas, newer RVs to transport us together, and

I'd noticed when Pops had started making bigger and more generous gifts to people in need. But as the show had grown, Pops had
been able to buy more and more rental properties. He continued
to be generous, often allowing several of his houses to be used by
friends or family at discounted rates, or even completely rent free.

It took a few days for the mist to clear and for us to suspect that
the money wasn't just a simple gift.

First, there was a comment from Pops about how none of us
needed to discuss the money with anyone else, either inside or outside the family: "If you have any issues, don't go stirring contention
among the brethren," he said. "You come to me."

A few weeks later the paperwork came through—a four-page
agreement emailed over by Chad. After having been tricked into
signing the previous contract, Derick and I were extra careful to
study this one, showing it to a lawyer, along with the portions of the
previous agreement we'd been given. If we were going to sign Pops'
new deal, we wanted to be clear about what we were giving up.

The contract wasn't with TLC or any other network. It was with
Mad Family Inc.—a company that Mom and Pops had previously
set up. In return for the eighty thousand dollars, for the next seven
years—plus an unlimited number of years beyond that if the company chose—we would have to commit to making not just ourselves
but our children, and any children yet to be born, available to any
show that Mad Family Inc. created or participated in. We would be
paid for that work as well, but at a rate that we would have to accept
without negotiation. We would also have to sign an NDA which
would remain active for the rest of our lives. Eighty thousand dollars
was a lot of money, but these strings were tight enough to choke.

Derick and I didn't even need a discussion. There was no way either of us were going to sign. Not that we told Chad or Pops that right away. We figured it would be wise to hold off on saying no to Pops until we absolutely had to.

Pops had been clear that we were not to talk about the deal with anyone else, either each other, our other siblings, or anyone outside the family. To me, at that time, the level of secrecy and control that Pops exerted on us felt normal. We had been conditioned to obey, and it wouldn't have occurred to me to see the hypocrisy in the fact that he would warn us against stirring up contention among the brethren while also using us against one another and duping us into signing contracts.

Most were scared enough of Pops' displeasure to obey, but not everyone did what he said. A few siblings asked us whether we were going to sign. I told them no, choosing my words carefully, fearful of stirring up family problems. I was surprised that almost everyone I spoke to felt fine about signing. Some said they had some edits they wanted to make to the agreement first, but I started to feel like they were being swept away by a soon-to-become treacherous river. I wanted to jump in and save them, but I wasn't sure I had that kind of power.

Signing a deal with Mad Family Inc. felt like jumping onboard a paper aircraft. Nothing about it felt safe. But that didn't mean we were down on Pops. Things weren't great between us, but it was late fall 2016 now and almost a year had passed since we had argued with him on the phone in El Salvador. We hadn't fought since then, and inside me there was just a small flame of hope that somehow, we might be able to build a stronger relationship in the future.

A few short weeks later, we were on a Duggar family trip in Branson, Missouri, at Thanksgiving when things changed. A month had passed since we'd been given the contract to sign, and Derick and I had been talking a lot and praying about everything that had been happening recently, trying to figure out how we could navigate things better with Pops. After getting some advice from an attorney outside the family circle of influence, Derick and I agreed that the next step would be to ask Pops to hand over a full copy of the contract that he'd had me sign the day before our wedding. He'd already sent us part of it in June, but seeing the whole thing felt like a good opportunity for him to be transparent and open with us. He was resistant. At least, he was playing the same stalling game on the 2014 contract that we were playing on Pops' eighty-thousand-dollar one. But on vacation, when we weren't all crowded on top of each other like we often were at home, there was an opportunity to talk with Pops face-to-face.

We were sitting a little removed from everyone else, at a table in an empty corner at Fritz's Adventure, a kids' climbing place in Branson, Missouri, when Pops walked over and sat down.

"I feel like there's still something between us," he said. There was a pause. Derick and I looked at each other.

"Well, yes," said Derick. "There's been some trust broken recently that might take a while to rebuild."

"It goes both ways. You've broken my trust too."

His stare was rock solid. I could taste the bile in my throat. I feared that things were about to get ugly again.

Then Pops surprised me. "I'm sorry," he said. I hadn't heard him say that many times before. The words sounded unfamiliar. But I liked them.

At least, I did until he finished his sentence.

"I'm sorry that I didn't let you know what you were obligated to."

"But Jill never read the contract she was signing, so she wasn't obligated to anything," said Derick, trying hard to hold his frustration in check. "Will you admit that?"

Pops shrugged. "Yeah, okay. I'm sorry for making her agree to something she wasn't obligated to."

"Thanks, Pops," I said. "We forgive y'all and love y'all too and really hope we can move forward and have great family relationships."

Later, when everyone was talking about what they were thankful for, I wondered what to say. I was thankful for Mom and I was thankful for Pops, too. I was thankful for my husband, my son, and the little life growing in my belly. But most of all, what I really wanted to say was that I was thankful for my husband and his bravery and courage despite the obstacles we had faced together that year. In all the stress of things with family, he was my biggest champion, and together we were learning to take back control of our lives, one small decision at a time.

The closer we got to the end of the year, the more pressure we came under to sign the agreement. We talked about it, prayed about it, and slept on it a whole lot. But even though Chad and Pops were persistent and persuasive, we just couldn't get any peace about signing anything at all. Yes, we wanted the money—even though it was nowhere near an accurate compensation for the hours and days and years spent filming—but we did not want to be tied up in any legal agreement with Pops to get it.

I guess Pops felt the same way, because in the last few days of December he visited us at home. I wanted to hide. I wanted everything to go away. I didn't want to have to pour concrete around my heart in an attempt to shield me from the blast.

But Pops wasn't there to fight. He was there to hand over a check for the full eighty thousand dollars. "What about the agreement?" Derick asked.

"I know y'all have been thinking over the contract and talking with Chad about revisions, and we had hoped to get all that wrapped up before the end of the year, but we can continue those conversations. Mom and I talked about this and we really want to go ahead and give y'all your payment now. We really love you guys."

"Thank you, Pops," I said. I meant it, but I wasn't rejoicing. Somehow it didn't feel like the end of the story.

Our return to El Salvador got pushed from December to February, thanks to a combination of filming commitments and safety concerns that Mike had. The time went quickly, and before we knew it, we only had a couple of weeks left in Arkansas. Aside from packing up and sourcing supplies that we wanted to take with us, there was one other task that we simply had to complete before we boarded the plane. We needed to find a lawyer.

Ever since *In Touch* magazine had published the story a year and a half earlier, my sisters and I had wanted to do what we could to right the wrongs legally and hopefully help protect other victims. We couldn't undo the damage and the pain that we had experienced, and the humiliation was unerasable. But hopefully we could get justice. We could hold to account the people who were complicit in the illegal release of documents relating to the investigation: Kathy O'Kelley; the City of Springdale, Arkansas; Washington County, Arkansas; Ernest Cate; Rick Hoyt; *In Touch* magazine and its parent company Bauer, and anyone else involved behind the scenes.

Pops had tried another law firm previously, but they didn't take the case. Now, in February 2017, time was against us. The statute of limitations was approaching, and we had to file by May. If we couldn't find a law firm to take us on, our window of opportunity would close forever. What made it even more of a challenge was the fact that none of us could afford to pay for it, even with Pops' eighty-thousand-dollar "gift." He offered to loan us the money, but I didn't feel at all good about being in debt to him. So we needed a firm that could take on local government, elected officials, and a national media organization, and do it contingency. It was a tall order, but thanks to a contact of my new brother-in-law, Jeremy, we found a firm in LA that thought we had a strong enough case and was willing to take a risk on us.

When Pops heard, he called me. The muscle memory was strong, and I braced for impact, worrying that he might be upset we hadn't included him or Chad in the process. But his voice was calm, his words genuine. "I'm so proud of you guys. I'm so glad you found somebody."

I exhaled a little with relief.

"But," he added, "I would be very careful about how you approach all of this. You know, we just got the show back up."

"Okay, Pops. Love you."

I was concerned about the show. I was concerned about Pops too. I didn't want to wreck the peace that was starting to form between us, as fragile and weak as it was. But I was relieved that my sisters and I had an attorney of our own to help us with this. LA was a long, long way from Arkansas, and for once I felt confident that Pops wouldn't be able to exert his control over the situation. Finally, we could fight for ourselves.

Soon after we arrived back in El Salvador we had a call with a large mission organization, the International Mission Board, or IMB, who we'd had a job interview with at a missionary expo—the same organization that Derick had previously worked with, and the one we had made contact with soon after our honeymoon. Their process was slow, requiring us to be a part of their church denomination for three years. With that hurdle finally cleared, we were beginning to have some more detailed conversations about us working with them.

The fact that we were already known through the show probably would have made a lot of organizations nervous about attracting too much attention to their sensitive work and pass us up, but the IMB was willing to look at us. And though being well known meant that some of our job options within this organization would be limited, we were excited. It felt like we'd found gold. We liked everything about them—their mission, their values, the way they operated and supported their missionaries—and had been so happy when they'd made the previous offer to join them. They sent missionaries all over the world, and they suggested we might either want to go to Spain or Panama.

Starting work with Mike after our initial interview with him had been pretty simple—all we'd needed to do was agree on the scope of the work, iron out a few details about funding and accommodation, and book our flights—but with IMB things were a bit different. It was a lot bigger, had been around over one hundred fifty years, and the steps we had to take were way more complex. There were training courses to attend, vetting procedures to pass, and interviews with potential mission partners to have. On average it took between two and four years to go from being accepted as a missionary to actually being sent out onto the mission field. We'd been working through it for a while, and we were finally deemed to be almost ready. Finally, we were able to let ourselves get excited about this new chapter opening up.

The call was pretty routine, but there was one question that caught us off guard.

"We just want to double check, is there anything that you guys can and can't do with the whole filming thing you do with your family, Jill?"

"You mean contractually?" I said.

"Yeah. Do you have any formal agreements that you've signed that would restrict your ability to be completely committed to your work?"

Derick and I squeezed hands, out of sight of the camera.

"Well, yes," he began. "There is an agreement Jill was tricked into signing the day before our wedding, but we don't feel obligated to it morally or legally because of the way the signature was gained."

There was a moment's silence. The man we were talking to looked confused.

Derick glanced at me. "We're happy to cut ties with anything filming related though, aren't we?"

I nodded. "We're ready to do that."

Then I reiterated, "We will quit the show right now to show you that we're serious about working with you."

"Well, okay then." The guy was smiling. "That's great. If you can provide us documentation that shows you're free from any contract, that will be just perfect."

It was strange to have talked about leaving the show with someone other than Derick. We had been speaking about it between ourselves for almost a whole year, and the timing felt right. But knowing that our secret was now out in the world, it felt strange. It felt dangerous. And it felt liberating, too.

All those whispered conversations between us about when we should leave the show had taken forever. Now that we had decided to leave, we needed to figure out how we were going to do it. And for that decision we didn't have the luxury of time. We needed to press on, to get things moving so that we could secure our release from the show in time to start our new post on the mission field within the next year.

We drafted two versions of the email. The first was a simple and clear resignation letter that we addressed to everybody we could think of at TLC and Discovery, the parent channel, and the production company. We gave them an end date of May 31, 2017, and said that we'd be back in Arkansas mid May and would make ourselves available to do any filming they wanted. We didn't copy Pops or Chad on it, because we wanted to convey that we were capable adults who could make decisions and communicate with the network for ourselves, plus go out as cleanly and with as little inter-ference as possible.

The second email we drafted to Chad.

We just wanted to let you know, after much prayer and consid-eration, to step back from the show. As of the end of May 2017, we feel like we're not supposed to be a part of the show anymore in any capacity.

We read and reread them both until I could recite them in my sleep. We talked long and hard about what might happen when we sent them. We talked about staying in our box, sticking firm to what we knew was the right thing for us to do. We talked and talked until there was nothing left to say.

I felt terrified. So terrified that I started having contractions. I had just entered my third trimester stretch at twenty-nine-weeks pregnant.

All I could do was breathe and hope that everything would work out all right.

Last minute, we decided it would be better and more respect-ful to call my parents first before the network, instead of emailing them. So, we prayed, picked up the phone, and, holding back tears, my stomach in knots, called my parents. They were both on the call. The tears started flowing and soaking the shirt that covered my pregnant belly as we let them know of our decision to quit filming at the end of May. I anticipated a difficult reaction or arguments, as we'd had in the past, but that didn't happen. We kept the call short. They were calm and didn't ask any questions. They didn't say much, but thanked us for letting them know.

After we hung up, we pressed send on the emails and waited.

The fallout was instantaneous. Chad emailed back demanding to know who else we had sent that email to. TLC emailed back too, wanting to talk. We told them that we were happy to have a call and share our side of the story. We wanted to explain how we'd been in the dark about things with the contract. At first they agreed, but then Chad must've gotten wind of the call, because they looped him in on the email thread—and all of a sudden the network wasn't allowed to talk with us unless Chad was on the call too.

From then on it was Groundhog Day: the same challenge over and over again. Every time we tried to get TLC to give us something that showed we were released from the contract, we hit a brick wall. We still only had a partial copy of the June 2014 contract, and neither Chad nor Pops would give us the full thing. Meanwhile, we were left trying to convince the IMB that the monthslong delay was only temporary and that soon enough we'd hopefully have the legal release they were requesting. About the only thing that appeared to be going well was my pregnancy. Those anxiety-inducing contractions had only lasted a day or so and not progressed into labor.

We tried to make the most of our last weeks in El Salvador. Despite all the Duggar-family mess and all the show-related chaos that we had experienced throughout our time there, we felt deeply connected to the people we had worked with. I had grown especially close with the pastor's wife, Maria. She was the sweetest, and I knew that she would always be there whenever I needed help. Leaving her and everyone else was going to be hard, especially as the security situation had deteriorated even further in the previous months.

Our former guard, German, was another of the friends we would miss the most. We had known him for a while, and he always helped to translate and make people laugh. His wife made the best choco-late, which we would buy whenever we needed a treat. He told us that his favorite meal was the hamburgers we'd cook him. German had been a member of MS-13, one of the brutal gangs responsible for so much of the killing in El Salvador. He had become a Chris-tian, and was a regular at church, but even that wasn't enough to keep his past from catching up with him. There were rumors that he was a target, and that if he carried on working with us, we would become a target too.

It was hard, but we knew that we had to let German go. We stayed in touch after he stopped working as our guard though, and he came to see us several times with his family.

One month before we were supposed to go back to the States, we got the call that German had been murdered.

Derick and I were stunned and devastated.

All the chaos and all the trauma that the show had thrown into our lives was nothing compared to German's murder. We had known the risks when we started our work in El Salvador, but a part of me never thought the danger would ever get so close to us.

The sorrow seemed to hang over the whole valley.

For weeks I felt empty inside.

Compared to the previous August, everything felt different when we flew back to northwest Arkansas in mid-May 2017. All my dials were turned up to the max—my anxiety about how people would respond to us, my fear that things with Pops were going to explode, my sense that we were returning to somewhere that felt less and less like home. The sadness I felt at leaving El Salvador weighed heavier in my heart than I thought possible.

We were both stressed about the ministry fundraising as well. Ever since we'd stood our ground about the promo shoot, it seemed to us that Chad's fundraising efforts had declined. We were still technically paying him 10 percent of anything raised, but barely any money was coming in. We still had our personal money, the eighty thousand dollars that Pops had paid us, but if we were going to be serious about life on the mission field, and still have some savings for our future, we needed a solid network of supporters. As we returned to Arkansas, our Dillard Family Ministry bank balance had fifteen hundred dollars in it.

There was frustration, too. We had been unable to secure any kind of document confirming our release from the show, and eventually the IMB could only wait so long. They reiterated to us that unless something changed with the contract deal in the next few months, we were in danger of losing the job opportunity we'd been wanting in Panama.

And yet, there was hope. Growing inside me, unaware of anything else in the world that might be troubling me or Derick, our second baby was thriving. I was very pregnant—over thirty-three weeks along now—and everything was looking good for the final weeks. In spite of all the stress and uncertainty around our future, there was one thing that we still agreed on with Mom and Pops: this new life we were about to welcome into the world was nothing less than a blessing.

With no job lined up and no knowledge of whether we would ever be able to get out of the contract, we battled hard to keep ourselves positive. Our little one—a boy—was due six weeks after we landed, and we would spend much of our time until then either getting ready for my sister Joy's upcoming wedding, or filming our final interviews for the show.

Of course, at some point someone from the show asked whether we would be willing to have cameras in when I went into labor.

We didn't need to think twice before answering them.

"Absolutely. No. Way," we said, on multiple occasions.

But there was a real curveball waiting for us, and it came from Chad. He informed us that he was no longer able to work with Dillard Family Ministries and was resigning from our board. That didn't surprise either of us at all, and it was kind of a relief. What troubled us was when we happened to check the balance on the ministry bank account. Chad had withdrawn almost all of it, leaving us with only a few hundred dollars in the ministry account that we used to pay ourselves a wage. We confronted him, and he gave us some story about a CPA bill being due even though what he was paid was supposed to cover those expenses.

The whole thing tasted bitter. Maybe another day we would have fought harder. But right then, with so much on our plate and with the future so full of unknowns, neither of us had the appetite for another battle. We just wanted to get through the next transition in our lives. There was just one last loose end to tie off before we were free. The show.

The producers asked if we could block out five hours so they could film some final exit interviews with us that they could use to tell viewers of our decision to leave the show. It seems strange to me now, but I don't remember much at all about the last interviews that

we filmed for *Jill & Jessa: Counting On*. I know what I was feeling—
a mix of sorrow and gratitude, of relief and anxiety, of feeling happy
that this was all behind us now at the same time as wondering what
was coming next—but I don't recall what we said. I remember them
asking us to give them a few different versions of our decision to
leave the show. I don't think any of it ended up making it into the
final cut of the show. Part of me still wonders why they didn't bother
to explain to viewers why we left. Part of me knows that it didn't
matter.

Other than that, as far as I recall, there was nothing to mark the
end of our involvement in the show. No speeches said and no final
paperwork that we had to complete. We just finished answering
whatever question we'd been asked, and the room fell into a brief
silence.

"That's it," said the cameraman.

We stood up from the couch where we'd been interviewed hun-
dreds of times before, in the shop building turned studio that sat
at the front of the Big House property. Nobody from my family
was there, so once we'd said our goodbyes to the film crew, we just
walked back to the car and drove home.

That was it.

For us, the show was over. We were out. Getting back onto the
mission field was harder than we'd hoped it would be, but at least
we were now free to do what we wanted. Free to relocate, to build
our lives the way we wanted them to be built, free to raise our boys
without any of the complications that I'd experienced. Part of me
was excited. Part of me found it more terrifying than anything I'd
ever encountered. Like a lifer who'd just been unexpectedly released,

I felt dazed and unsure about this new world ahead of me. It was all too vast. All too unknowable. I was just twenty-six years old.

Derick held me close those nights, him, me and the little one pushing the skin so tight across my belly that you could see the outline of the little foot or elbow was on the other side.

"You see," said Derick whenever our baby in utero would kick and squirm. "Everything's going to be all right."

———∞∞∞———

CHAPTER SEVEN

Dying. Inside and Out

All my life I'd been taught that suffering was good. For anyone doing the Lord's work, pain was to be accepted, even embraced. "Many are the afflictions of the righteous," I was told often by my parents, quoting Psalms 34:19. "But the LORD delivereth him out of them all." And I believed them. When people criticized us in the press, it was a sign the ministry was working. When filming was hard and demanding, it was a privilege to serve the Lord. Even when it felt like the whole world was peering at us through paparazzi lenses, there was a voice inside me saying, *Tough it out, Jill, this is what it means to serve God.*

As my final weeks of pregnancy became a regular roll call of aches and pains and reflux and insomnia and swollen ankles and everything else besides, I smiled. *Tough it out, Jill, this is what it means to be a mama.*

My water broke while Derick and I were out on a triple date, having ice cream at Cold Stone Creamery with Mom, Pops, and some friends. We rushed back home. I used my midwife doppler device to listen to the baby's heartbeat: 154 bpm with good variability. His head was engaged, and his position was good. Everything was looking great.

Thirty-six hours later, I was a long way from great. The contractions were about two minutes apart and I was fully dilated. I'd only been pushing for about half an hour, when the baby stopped descending. The pain had been excruciating until I'd been given an epidural, but I was losing all my energy to push. I was feeling weak and tired. I tried to summon that voice that would tell me to tough it out, but it was on mute.

"I can't." That was all I could say.

"C'mon, Jill," came the doctor's voice beside the bed. I kept my eyes closed, not really wanting to see what kind of stern look I was getting. She'd been with me for a while now, and the more tired I'd gotten the more assertive her voice had become. "Let's roll you over on the other side. You've got another contraction coming, Jill. You have to push for me, okay?"

When it hit, I tried to push, but I had nothing to give. It was all I could do to breathe. I drifted.

For a moment, I was left alone. I could hear voices talking, but they were a soft blur. If I retreated far enough into myself, I could block everything out.

"Jill," said the doctor. Her voice was different now. Still assertive, but there was another note in there now too. She was concerned. "Listen to me, Jill. Baby's heart rate isn't recovering as quick as we'd like it to after the contractions. It's dipping to seventy and not coming up fast enough. We need to get this baby out now. With this next contraction, you have to push. You know this stuff, Jill. You know what this means."

I knew what it meant. It meant the baby was potentially in distress. It meant that something was wrong.

"Okay," I said.

Then the doctor changed her mind. "Nope!"

I looked up and saw the doctor standing at the end of my bed. "We're doing a C-section, *now!* Prep for surgery!"

For a few seconds I was aware of the room exploding into action as the bed was pulled out from the wall and broken down to become a gurney.

Then came the pain. And the screaming. I realized after a minute it was my own.

I felt as if someone had just sliced me open on my side. I looked down, half expecting to see blood. There was none. But the pain was like nothing I'd ever known.

Then it hit me—I'd had an epidural. If the pain was strong enough to break through drugs that strong, something was seriously wrong.

My screams only got louder.

I felt sick, the kind of sick that seeped into every muscle and every organ. I shut my eyes as I kept screaming. I could vaguely sense motion. Felt a breeze on my face as the bed hurtled down the corridor. But it might as well have been happening to someone else. Besides the sound of screaming, the only thing that existed for me was the pain in my side, a ripping and a tearing unlike anything I could ever imagine.

The lights were bright in the OR. The doctor was gowned, but I could see the concern in her eyes as she leaned over.

"Jill, the anesthetist isn't here yet, but we can't wait. I'm going to have to start without him."

I could still hear my screams as the doctor started giving me shots of local anesthetic and began slicing me open to get to the baby as soon as possible. I heard someone else shouting about the amount of blood I was losing and another person yelling as they counted every instrument and item the doctor put inside me. But another thought within me was even louder. *This is it, Jill. This is where you and the baby die. This is the end. There's no more need to tough it out.*

I opened my eyes to see Derick. He was wearing the same shirt that he'd been wearing for the past two days, but he looked five years older. His eyes, though, were relieved.

I wanted to ask what happened, but the pain silenced me. It wasn't just on my side now, but all down my lower torso.

"Four hours," he said, holding my hand. His voice was shaky, as if he'd just that minute stepped out from a car wreck. "You've been out for four hours, but it's okay. You're okay. You had a uterine rupture. There was a hole in it. It was as big as my first. You lost a lot of blood, too, about half your total blood volume. But they gave you a transfusion and they were able to keep your uterus. You're going to be okay, Jill. They saved your life," Derick said with tears in his eyes.

"The baby?"

"The baby's okay, Jill. They had to take him to a different hospital. But he's in the NICU there."

For all the pain, the ache of my baby not being at my side was the worst. I trusted the decision the staff had taken to transfer him to a better NICU, but I wanted to hold my baby. I *needed* to hold him, to feed him and care for him. Being separated like that was like they'd taken away my heart and lungs. I couldn't last long with *that* kind of rupture within me.

It was four days before I was released from my hospital and finally met my baby—whom we named Samuel—face-to-face for the first time. The days that followed were all compressed into one big blur of nighttime pumpings and getting up and down to the NICU to feed and hold Samuel. My mom was with me all the time, and she made sure Derick and I were taken care of. Derick had gotten some video of the birth, but I couldn't watch it. Samuel had been unresponsive at birth. He'd been oxygen-deprived for a little while during the rupture and swallowed some meconium. When he came out, he had been limp in the nurse's hands. When I finally got to hold him in the NICU, I experienced the slow, dawning realization of just how close Samuel and I had both come to death.

Samuel made some improvement in the NICU, but there were still enough concerns about what he'd been through for him to be sent for a scan. It revealed signs of bleeding on the brain.

"There's nothing we can do about it right now," a doctor told us as we sat beside the ultraviolet glow of Samuel's incubator. "All we can do is follow up with another scan in a few months to see how he's healing. It's only then that we'll be able to begin to understand whether there's any damage to the brain."

It was a shock to hear this, but there was nothing we could do but accept it. Our entire world had been shaken by the birth.

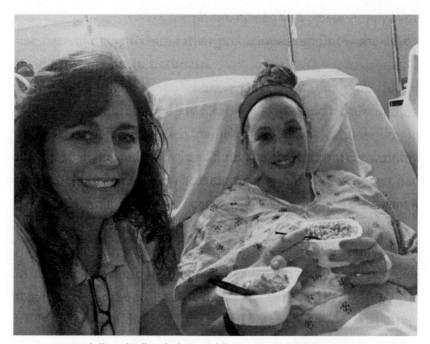

Michelle with Jill at the hospital following Samuel's birth, July 2017

Everything was in the air. There were no guarantees for whatever was coming next.

After a total of nine days in the NICU we were released to go home, with several follow-up appointments scheduled in the coming days and weeks. My world was small in those days, with room for me to only focus on Samuel, Derick, and Israel. Everything else—from what I was going to eat that day to what our lives would look like now that we'd left the show—it all floated beyond me like ocean mist. And that was okay. Thanks to my mom, Jessa, Jana, Anna, Joy, my other little sisters, my grandma Mary, Aunt Deanna, lots of friends from our church, Derick's brother, Dan, and his wife, Deena, and Derick's mom, Cathy, I could forget about food and laundry and everything else entirely. I appreciated their love and support more than I ever thought possible.

But even when life was as fragile as it was in those days, the show still had a way of casting its cold, dark shadow over us. Derick stepped out from the NICU one afternoon to see Pops there, talking with some of the staff. Derick was confused, as with hospital protocol only allowing a limited number of slots on our unsupervised visitor list, we'd not given Pops permission to visit. Thanks to the show, however, everyone knew who Pops was. When he'd come for a visit, he'd been invited inside without hesitation.

We were on better terms with Pops at the time, but still cautious around him. Nevertheless, Derick didn't make a big deal of Pops charming his way in as a visitor, and chatted with him about Samuel's progress.

"A lot of people are asking about him," said Pops, holding his phone so Derick could glance at it.

There was a text message that had just come in from Chad, who was still working with Pops:

Get me a picture of that baby!

Derick was fuming. He took out his own phone and messaged Chad soon after. *Please do not ask other people for pictures of my children. It makes me uncomfortable. Thank you.*

Chad responded five minutes later.

I haven't asked anyone for pictures of your children. I have no idea what you're talking about.

Samuel still needed oxygen when he was nine days old, but there was no need for him to be in an incubator or even in the NICU, so they sent him home with a little oxygen tank and nasal tube. It was a relief, and with the sun shining and the four of us Dillards finally able to sleep under the same roof and eat around the same table, it felt like life was starting over.

I knew the healing would take time, but people were kind and supportive and made sure that I didn't do anything that put too much strain on me. I was especially grateful that Mom had taken me for the traditional pre-birth manicure and pedicure that she tries to do for all us girls before we have a baby. I was in the middle of my postpartum period, cocooned away at home and still on painkillers as my C-section wound was knitting itself together, but looking at my nice nails made me smile. It reminded me that I had good people out there who loved and cared for me. I was so grateful to Mom and everyone who was helping, but I noticed that Derick was feeling pretty drained. He'd just been through a long period of shuttling between home and various hospitals, and then of looking after Israel, worrying about me and Samuel, all the while still feeling stunned and shocked by the birth itself. He needed a break.

My younger brother Joseph was getting married, and his bachelor party out on Beaver Lake was just a few days after our return home from the hospital. Derick had grown up on the same lake, and if ever there was a time for him to take the day off and enjoy some male company, this was it. The only drawback was that it was going to be filmed. We weren't opposed to Derick being on-camera, though we really didn't know how it would feel to be there around everyone in light of us leaving the show. We had no regrets at all about leaving the show, but we were realistic about the place that filming had in Duggar family life. If we were going to see my family, we knew most of the time we'd have to do it with cameras present.

We talked and prayed about it a lot and reached a place where we felt good and peaceful about being at the bachelor party, but with Samuel and I not being filmed. It felt like we would be gaining back control.

Derick's mom took Israel, and we headed over to the lake. We intentionally got there a little late, after they'd filmed a lot of what they needed. I sat on the dock in the shade, far behind the film crew. It was good to see Derick having fun, waterskiing and just hanging out like he had often done with his family growing up, and the sound of his laughter was better than any painkiller. Marrying into the Duggar family had cost him more than I think either of us could have imagined, but it wasn't as if the family was all bad. Far from it. Derick was loved by so many of my brothers and sisters, and it was important to remember that.

That day on the lake was the first time that I'd seen the crew since leaving the show, and it was good to know that there were no hard feelings. We talked a little and joked about the guys on their water skis. I introduced them to Samuel but saw the way some of them did a double take when they saw the little oxygen tube running underneath his nose.

"How's he doing?"

"He's doing great. Just needs a little oxygen right now, but he's doing great." I knew that I was deliberately holding back the full story, not because I didn't trust the crew, but because that story was still so unformed. We didn't know the extent of any brain damage and had no idea what Samuel's future would be like. There was a chance that he'd have significant learning difficulties, but there was no way of telling now. So, Derick and I decided that we would keep things to ourselves for now. At least until we knew more and could make a better decision. We were going to protect him. I was going to give Samuel what I didn't have myself when I was younger.

With Samuel, we prepared for the long haul. We'd been told that it would take a year and a half at least for any developmental problems to start to emerge, maybe longer. But the scan that was booked for when he reached three months still felt significant, and we drove the three hours to Little Rock that fall, hoping that nothing dramatic would show up.

That evening after Samuel's MRI, just after we made it back home, my phone rang. It was the neurologist.

We'd been told that it would likely take a few days before the report would be sent over from the radiologist to the neurologist to read, and then they'd call us with the results, so we weren't expecting a call yet at all.

"Doctor?" I said, putting the neurologist on speaker.

"I wanted to call you myself as soon as I read the report," she said. "I don't get to make these calls very often. What I've seen on the scans is a miracle. There's no lasting damage at all."

I let out a cry of amazement. Derick was quiet with shock.

"Usually, I'd expect to see some scarring after a bleed like that. But on Samuel's scans there's nothing. Everything is healed. That doesn't mean he won't have any lasting issues. We're still gonna want to evaluate him every three months until he's around two years old. But if he gets to that point and he's walking and talking and doing all the things we'd expect him to be doing by then, we won't need to see him anymore."

It was like we'd been released from death row. The air tasted sweeter, and the sky looked bigger. The future felt brighter and more hopeful than it had for months.

Our application to go back out on the mission field was still on hold until we could get the official release from the show, but our desire to serve overseas was just as strong as ever. Derick had decided to enroll in a one-year ministry residency program, partially funded and run by our church. We figured it would give us something to do during the time that we were waiting and would add more ministry skills, seminary hours, ministry licensure and experience that would be valuable in the future. As a bonus, the school offered housing, which meant we could finally have our own space and put a little more physical distance between us and the family.

A month after Samuel had been born, we'd moved out into the church rental duplex thirty minutes away from the Big House. I'd been unable to lift anything, but thankfully, my family was still there to help. The army of Duggar siblings and Derick packed us up and moved all our stuff.

Since our return from El Salvador, we'd been living in a house that Grandma Duggar owned—a 4,400-square-foot, two-story home set on one and a half acres with farmland views. Our new place was a 1970s two-bed, two-bath duplex that had a hornet nest by the back step, occasional visits from garter snakes, and mice in the kitchen. But despite the infestations we were happy in the new house. There were other ministry students nearby, and we were looking forward to building new relationships with our new community. We were our own family, finally free to be who we wanted. This—I told my-self so many times during those long August days when Derick was away working with the church and I was with the two boys in the house—this was the point when, finally, our new life would begin.

Trouble was, moving on and letting go of the past was an im-possible task. It didn't matter how much Derick and I talked about building our lives together, what future I dreamed of, or how badly I wanted to begin again, I felt stuck. I felt like I was in chains, and I couldn't break free from the past. My heart was open to the possi-bility of a new life, but my head was full of reasons why I couldn't. For every whisper of hope, there was an avalanche of guilt. For every moment of joy, there was a stab of fear.

I had IBLP to thank for that particular baggage. Ever since I was a kid, every decision I'd made had been gripped with a level of guilt or fear that weighed heavy in my decision-making. Over time I'd gotten so used to it that I hardly noticed it was there. But now that I'd walked away from the family ministry and we were beginning to change in other areas, I couldn't just ignore it.

At first, the guilt manifested itself around children, specifically whether I would be physically able to have any more. As my body started to heal, my mind became troubled. Having just had my sec-ond C-section and experienced a uterine rupture—not to mention Samuel's stroke and brush with death—I was just waking up to the possibility that I might not be able to have any more kids. It was not an easy thing for me to accept, despite the fact that I had been doing a lot of questioning about IBLPs teaching over the years. In 2014 Mr. Gothard had stepped down after being accused of sexual harassment and molestation by thirty-four women. It was the year

Derick and I married, and I'd started questioning the IBLP view of scripture. The closer I'd looked at the Bible, the more it seemed to contradict what I had been taught as a child, especially the idea that adult children were still under their parent's authority, and the way they had placed Mr. Gothard on a pedestal. But one thing I hadn't thrown out was the belief that children are a blessing. Before I got married, I knew that I wanted to have as many children as I possibly could. Becoming a mama had only strengthened that belief within me. But after Samuel's birth, there was a very real chance that he would be my last child.

All of this was stirring within me when Derick and I made a trip back to the hospital one day. For once it was nothing to do with Samuel or me—we were visiting a family friend who'd just had a baby. I was surprised to see Mom and Pops there, but it was good to catch up, especially on safe, neutral ground like that.

We all had to step outside for a moment while the staff did something in the room. Mom and Pops, Derick, me, and another friend of mine were all standing in the corridor together when my friend leaned close and asked me about Samuel.

"How're you doing?" she whispered. "You healing up?"

I'd been guarded about Samuel, carefully keeping the story about his birth to only the closest people around me. I didn't want him to become a storyline in anyone's tabloid, but I trusted my friend.

"Kinda," I said, keeping my voice low. "But it was rough. I don't know whether I'm going to be able to have any more kids."

My friend reached out to put an arm around me, but before she could say anything, Pops' voice filled the corridor.

"We don't know for sure now, do we?"

I turned. He was looking right at me, smiling. He meant well, I guess, but in that moment I was mad. I wanted to ask him why he thought he had the right to comment about my uterus, but I bit the words back.

The moment passed, and I doubt that either my friend or Pops would even remember it. But I did. It was triggering. It hit a nerve in me, invalidated my feelings and pressed on the bruise of my guilt—a bruise that had formed after Israel's birth. Even though contraceptives were generally not allowed in IBLP, I'd used birth control after having the C-section with him, knowing that all medical advice recommended not getting pregnant for about eighteen months after the operation. Even though Derick and I had prayed about it. Even though we had agreed as a couple that it wasn't wrong for us to use non-abortive contraception and we knew we were making healthy choices, that didn't lessen the guilt I felt, because it went against the way I was raised. Yet it was a decision that had caused me no end of guilt, and I'd kept it secret from nearly everyone, apart from Derick. Now, after Samuel, not getting pregnant wasn't a matter of choice. There was a chance that perhaps my body simply wouldn't be able to sustain another pregnancy, that I would never be able to give birth again. It was earth shattering, and the prospect left me traumatized.

And so, the fearful thoughts began.

I've always imagined myself having a ton of kids, but what would my life look like if I could only have two children?

Do I really believe what I was taught, that even if the doctors told me not to, a godly woman should question the doctor's opinion and be willing to try for more kids in most cases and trust that God would protect her?

I'd always been taught that most people who were saying they'd stopped having children on the advice of their doctor were using it as a cop-out. IBLP's view was that a lot of people with small families were basically lazy. Feeling overwhelmed, stressed out, or like you couldn't cope with having more kids was no excuse. In fact, the only acceptable approach to the matter was to leave the decision up to God and trust that he would provide the grace required to cope. Anyone who wasn't coping just wasn't relying on God fully enough.

What if old friends start to ask questions and notice the gap between our kids? What if they figure out we're using contraception, or guess that something might be wrong?

It turns out that living with fearful thoughts is a lot like living with hornets and garter snakes. Once they find a way in, you can block as many holes as you like, but the struggle to keep them out will require constant vigilance. And when they do get in—which they will—the memory of all those previous attacks will make whatever you're facing so much worse.

I used to think I might not be able to handle all the kids God gave me. Was this his way of answering that? I felt conflicted. I was devastated at the thought of not being able to have more kids, and I felt like my fertility had been robbed from me. But also, dare I say it, I was somewhat relieved. The devastation far outweighed the relief, but there was a small part of me that appreciated the excuse not to have to go through a zillion pregnancies and deliveries. I always liked getting to the stage where I could feel the baby move and listen to the heartbeat, but with both the boys my first trimesters had been rough, leaving me bedridden with nausea.

My inward critic told me not to feel sorry for myself. I knew that others outside the insular world I grew up in wouldn't understand this conflict. They might even tell me to just be happy with the two kids I had.

But in my world, big families were everywhere. If you didn't have one, then there was probably something wrong with your body. I hated that I could still feel the involuntary recoil at the stigma.

I had always been told that we should "trust God with the size of our families," and "have as many kids as God would give us." Even when I heard this, way before Derick and I were married, it seemed hard to swallow at the time. I dared not speak it, but the thought was always there in the back of my head that I didn't know if I could physically and emotionally handle that many pregnancies and deliveries. But I figured if that was God's plan for my life, then I shouldn't question it. Sweet Jilly Muffin should just accept it and trust that God would somehow provide the grace to get through it.

When it came to trusting God with the size of your family, there was one phrase that I heard often—that "God opens and closes the womb." Growing up, I guess I'd always focused on the idea of God opening the womb and pouring out his blessings on us. I'd liked that idea a lot. But now it felt like God was closing me up. I wasn't so sure I was okay with that.

What if trusting God doesn't only mean trusting him with more kids than I feel I'm able to handle? What if it means being content with only two kids?

That was never part of my plan.

At some point, I started to try and tune out the anxiety. My feelings on the matter were so complicated, and I knew I had a whole lot of sorting out to do. I didn't know what the future held, but I was relieved that we didn't have to make any decisions right now. And I was even more thankful that God had led us to step away from the show when he did. I was so glad we were able to protect Samuel while we waited to learn more, but I also was thankful that I had time to process everything without having to rehash it all in an interview chair for the show multiple times, stumbling over my words and still in the midst of working through it—only for strangers to critique while I processed everything, further adding to my trauma.

Fertility wasn't the only complicated area in my life at the time. Friendship and community brought its own challenges. Derick was out most days working in international college ministry on the University of Arkansas campus, or at the church, taking classes as part of the ministry program, keeping the car with him. The other young families from the church lived nearby, but I still felt lonely and isolated. We were just thirty minutes away from the Big House, but my siblings didn't come by a whole lot. I still wanted to hang out, and I'd see them from time to time if I made my way over there and hung out awhile, but it was just to be around them and pretend like everything was all good. I didn't feel like we were on the same playing field anymore. They were living the life I used to live, and I had chosen to move on. Sometimes it was a hard reality to be faced with.

I wanted to reach out to people beyond my family, to sit and talk just like I'd been able to do with the moms down in El Salvador, but it was different. Down in El Salvador, there was no risk in me talking with other moms about the dangers I was facing—we were all at risk in some way from the gangs. I could be real with them and they could be real with me. I missed that freedom and comfort, and I missed the way my faith felt strengthened just by being in their company. Down there, the women in the church—like the pastor's wife Maria—were like giants, trusting God in the face of so much adversity. They were like big sisters to me, and I missed them so much.

Back in Arkansas, there was no way I could talk about my fear, and my faith was feeling shaken. All the times I'd been warned not to "stir up contention among the brethren" had left their mark on me. I was hardwired not to be critical of my parents to anybody—not my siblings, not my pastor, and certainly not to my friends. The thought of doing it nauseated me.

From the guilt, the fear grew.

The spotlight that the show had placed on our family meant that people were always assuming things about us or itching to be the first to report anything negative. I could see it in people's eyes, hear it in their questions.

"Do you miss the show?"

"I guess you've got a ton of babysitters on hand with your family living round here!"

"Are there any new courtships happening in the new season?"

Even something as simple as, "How are your parents? Tell them we say hey!" felt dangerous. Every interaction with someone outside the family had me on alert, just like it had since the early days of the show, when we'd have to remind people not to post anything on social media if they'd been around us while we were filming. A few times stories had leaked out about upcoming weddings or relationships, and we'd spend time trying to figure out who had leaked the info. It was hard to shake off that kind of suspicious mindset, and as I tried to make a new life for myself and build new friendships with people, I'd often wonder what their agenda was, or how likely they would be to sell anything I told them to the tabloids. Growing up Duggar had left me paranoid about people.

"Remember," Pops would say again and again whenever we were talking about the show, "other people don't really understand, and they might be jealous. Let's not talk about this with anybody else."

I had been trained to keep all interactions with people outside the show as light and superficial as possible. Even when there were no cameras, if we were among people who were not immediate family, I was playing my role. I'd smile, keep everything positive, just like I did when we were filming. Only when the doors at the Big House were closed could I relax and be myself, whoever she was.

At home with Samuel and Israel, while Derick was out at work, I'd try to talk with some of the other mamas from church. I'd do okay if the conversation was light and easy, but the minute anyone asked me how I was doing, I'd feel the emotion start to whirl within me. I knew that if I even came close to trying to answer them, I'd wind up sobbing, and that was terrifying. My emotional muscle memory took over, and I filtered my words like I was making baby formula. I kept everything spotless. There was a block against any hint of grit or dirt about Duggar family life passing my lips.

I hated it.

At the time when I needed friendships the most, I realized that I didn't know how to talk to people. Sweet Jilly Muffin had been a gold star kid in the Big House, but out in the world without any Duggars around, she was just a hollow, lonely, scared girl.

I was caught in no-man's-land, that strange space between the foreign enemy on one side and the safety of home on the other.

Only, for me, the roles were reversed. Home (the Big House) was where the risk was, while the strangers were my hope for safety. I guess I wanted the freedom to follow where we were feeling called, to a world beyond my family and the way I'd been raised. I just didn't have either the tools or the guide to help me do it and survive.

The one place I felt like I could relax was church. I cherished Sundays, and not just because Derick would be with me much of the day. He'd drive us to the campus, and we'd join the flow of people making their way through the doors and into the auditorium. With a couple thousand other people in attendance, I could feel myself relax as I blurred into the crowd.

Church was nothing like IBLP. There was no Mr. Gothard figure at the center, drawing attention to himself. There were no Model Families brought up onstage to give us a model of perfection to emulate. They didn't even use the King James version of the Bible. They didn't talk about authority in the same way I'd heard it taught, they didn't say how important it was that children obeyed their parents far into adulthood, and they didn't preach that women should wear dresses at all times. Instead, they talked about Jesus, love and grace. They still talked about God's holiness, justice, and our need for sanctification, but it was different than many of the rules I'd been taught in IBLP. They were genuine about wanting to build community with young couples and families, and the result was captivating. To people in IBLP, it might have been "a worldly church," or as my dad once said, "a two-kid church." To me, it looked like a healthy church with a more balanced view of freedom in Christ.

I know that no church is perfect, but I wasn't looking for perfection. I spent a lot of time studying people there, not so that I could start following them. I was just aware of the contrast. IBLP families tended to dress, speak and smile the same, but in our new church there was a big range of people and behaviors to observe. A few of the older men might wear ties, but most people dressed like they were just heading out to the mall. A bunch of men and women had tattoos, and women of all ages—including the pastor's wife—wore pants. One of the women on the worship team even had a nose ring. But nobody looked like they were doing any of this out of rebellion or to particularly draw attention to themselves. In fact, me sitting there in my ankle-length skirts and covered shoulders made me stand out way more than anyone else.

"Derick," I said one Sunday afternoon when we'd gotten back from church and the boys were both taking a nap. "What do you think about pants?"

He was watching a replay of an OSU game, so all I got was a "Huh?"

"Do you think that it makes guys think bad thoughts?"

"What?"

"Women wearing pants. I was always taught it was a sin."

He pressed pause. "Well, no. I don't think it is."

"But Deuteronomy 22:5."

He looked blank.

" 'The woman shall not wear that which pertaineth unto a man, neither shall a man put on a woman's garment: for all that do so are an abomination unto the LORD thy God.' Growing up I was always told this verse meant that women shouldn't wear pants because they were originally designed for men, and men shouldn't wear skirts because they were women's clothing."

Someone scored and he zoned out for a moment. "Well, maybe these days skirts are women's clothing, but back in that culture, men wore robes which were basically skirts. Seeing a woman wearing pants doesn't make me have bad thoughts."

"That's just because you're used to it."

"But what about James 4:17, 'To him who knows what to and does it not, to him it is sin.'" My parents would say that because I have been taught the dangers of dressing immodestly and wearing pants, that it would be especially sinful for me, because I "know better." They'd say I would be lowering my standards.

"Are we talking about personal convictions or hard-line sin issues? Because there is a difference. If it's a hard-line sin issue, then it would be a sin for everyone."

The discussion was over and Derick went back to his highlights. I kind of agreed with him about the rule belonging to another culture, but I was kind of annoyed with him as well. It wasn't fair, but somewhere deep inside of me there was a part that wanted Derick to tell me that pants were wrong, just like Pops always had. Growing up, having the world divided into *thou shalls* and *thou shalt nots* by Pops or IBLP ideology made life appear easier. I had grown up believing that if I just followed the rules, I would be okay. I guess that belief started to crumble when I learned that Pops had manipulated me into signing the contract. Maybe authority wasn't always totally trustworthy.

Instead of just getting Derick to decide for me, I thought over our conversation and decided to pray and study the issue more myself. I looked at the Bible to see what else it said about women in pants (turns out not so much) and looked past the style choices of the pastor's wife and the worship leader and decided that I liked, admired, and respected them. The more I talked with them, the more I could see that they were both godly women who just happened to wear pants and a nose ring. It didn't define them.

One thing about pants kept on troubling me though. Even if I didn't think they were sinful, there was the bigger issue of my parents' wishes to consider. If I started wearing pants, it would likely be seen as an act of rebellion against them, and I really didn't want to be viewed that way by either my parents or the press. The way I saw it, I was already in enough spiritual peril without adding another potential judgment onto my back.

Then, just as I was feeling like there was no way to untie this knot, something happened that was shocking to the Duggar fan base and made tabloid headlines. My sister Jinger decided to start wearing pants. Not on the show, and not at the Big House, but whenever she was back home in Texas with her husband, Jeremy.

I waited for the fallout. I watched the family text message groups— at least the ones that I had not been removed from—wondering how long it would take Pops to call her out or cut and paste that verse from Deuteronomy. But nothing happened that I was aware of. There was no public condemnation, no backhanded shaming.

One day I called Jinger. She told me that she'd faced some backlash behind closed doors, but encouraged me to make good decisions, not based out of fear of what others would think.

Jinger's decision to think for herself while staying true to the Bible was inspiring. Derick and me trying to figure out what we believed together in other areas too was difficult but comforting. All my life I'd followed the IBLP teaching that drinking alcohol was a sin. I knew there was truth to the real dangers with getting drunk and had always been warned about the slippery slope. But after studying what the Bible says about it I resolved that it wasn't a sin for me to drink, though for a long time I was still afraid to try it. Eventually, the thought of an occasional relaxing date while sipping a glass of wine with my hubby sounded lovely. After long conversations with Derick and setting some clear, healthy boundaries ahead of time for ourselves, I was nervously excited when Derick brought back a bottle of wine to accompany our in-home date night one evening.

But I didn't like it. It made my mouth feel like it had just been disinfected. I was kind of disappointed.

When Samuel's oxygen tank was no longer needed, and I was finally feeling like I was fully healed, we decided to celebrate with our first big family day out. It was just Derick, the boys and me, plus Cathy and her husband, Ronnie, and Derick's brother and his wife. There was only one place I wanted to go—a theme park in Branson, Missouri, called Silver Dollar City.

Growing up, I always got excited when I heard that we were going to Silver Dollar City. From the moment we woke up and all throughout the two-hour drive there, my siblings and I would talk about which rides we were going to tackle first and how wet we'd get on American Plunge. We'd drive back happy, exhausted, and grateful for the small fortune it had cost our parents to take us there.

On the fall morning that we were due to go, I felt different. The excitement was there, but so were the nerves. I'd decided that since it was going to be cold and I'd be on the rides, it wasn't the day for dresses. I'd picked out a pair of leggings that I sometimes wore under a skirt, found a long T-shirt that covered my butt, and a coat that covered the T-shirt. I'd decided that this was the day that I would first wear pants, but now that I had them on, I just felt wrong. Even without the guilt and the fear, I felt like nothing was going to look good on my post pregnancy, breastfeeding body.

"What do you think?" I asked Derick just before his mom arrived.

"It's fine," he said, checking his watch.

"No, I'm wearing pants, Derick."

He paused and looked at me. "You look great. And it's practical too. You'll be fine."

We arrived at the park and I tried to breathe deep and not think about anything but the rides. Israel was just big enough to go on the smaller ones, and it was fun watching him get all excited and wide-eyed as we walked around—him skipping on ahead, me with my coat belted tight. I was just starting to relax a little, when someone came up and asked me for a picture. This happened a lot, and I'd always said yes in the past. But now? For a moment I wondered what it would be like to say no, but I didn't want to be that person. So I smiled, tried to pull my coat down as far as possible, and kind of hoped that it wouldn't end up getting tagged on Facebook.

We must have been there an hour or two when I saw something in the distance that made me reach for Derick's hand.

"My family," I said, my voice shaky and my heart racing. "Look!"

The Duggar clan had just arrived. Mom and Pops, Jana and

nearly every other sibling that was still living at home, ready for the thrills of a day at Silver Dollar City.

There was no TV crew with them, and I knew I couldn't hide from them for the whole day, that sooner or later we'd run into one another. But I decided to try all the same and steered us Dillards quickly off in the opposite direction.

The rest of the day was a series of near misses. I was feeding Samuel when a couple of my siblings saw me and came over to say hi. Luckily, I was sitting down and had a nursing cover draped around me so my bottom half was kind of invisible. I came within twenty yards of Mom and Pops while we were both in line for different rides. We said hi, and I was grateful for the low hedge that separated us and covered my legs. By the time we got in the car to drive home, I was way more exhausted than I'd ever been as a kid. Of all the days I could have decided to wear pants for the first time, I happened to have picked that one. I was so frustrated, and wished the whole thing hadn't been such a big deal for me.

I guess it was inevitable that the person who took the photo would post it on Facebook, that they would tag me, and that various sites would pick it up and that it would trigger one of the Google alerts that Pops had set up to monitor anything and everything posted about the family. From that point on, it was inevitable that he would say something to me.

"Jill? Can I talk to you upstairs?"

It was a few days after that Silver Dollar City trip, and I was over at the Big House. Mom wasn't there, neither was Derick. I followed

Pops up to his and Mom's bedroom, the scene where all the most serious conversations always took place.

He looked calm, but there was an edge to his voice that made me nervous. "Were you wearing pants the other day?"

"Well, not exactly." My stomach felt like it was about to explode. "They were leggings. So, um, yeah? Kind of." I was twenty-six, but Pops was looking at me like I was twelve again.

Pops stood up started pacing. Never a good sign.

"You know, Jinger called and talked with us about her decision before she started wearing pants." The words stung. Even though she'd told me that they'd given her a hard time too, I felt like he was finding me guilty of a double sin—not just wearing pants, but failing to meet the standards Jinger had set when she told them.

"Jinger took the time to go through the Bible and explain to us how she was feeling about it all. You know, Mom's got this book somewhere that talks a lot about clothing and modesty and what it does to men when they see women wearing pants and stuff. So maybe you should give that a read."

"Great," I said, wanting to get out of the room as soon as possible. "Thank you, Pops."

I took the book, knowing that if I decided to read it, it likely wouldn't change anything.

I cried when I got home. I felt embarrassed, humiliated, even though nobody else had been in the room with us. Pops had told us ever since we were little that we needed to be able to stand up for our convictions, even if others disagreed. Why couldn't he see that by deciding to wear pants, I was doing exactly what he'd taught us?

All my life I'd been trying to show respect to Pops, but when was he going to show the same to me?

Some people thought that I was just trying to prove something to my parents. Some people thought I was deliberately rebelling. The truth is that I thought pants looked good and were comfortable to wear. I felt the same way about nose piercings too, which in many ways were even considered worse than pants as they were an "ungodly distraction." But I thought they were cute. There was a worship leader at church who had hers done, and I thought it looked good on her. That's why, a short time after escaping from Pops' room, I woke up one morning and just knew that was going to be the day I would make my first-ever visit to a tattoo parlor and get my nose ring.

Taking a lesson from Jinger, I called Pops and Mom first. Pops' phone went to voice mail, which was a relief, and I kept my message as brief and courteous as possible. Mom picked up, but aside from thanking me for letting her know, she didn't have much to say.

The piercing itself was uneventful.

The voice mail that was waiting for me from Pops when I got out . . . that was another thing altogether. He pleaded with me not to do it. He told me I was making a huge mistake. He begged me to think about how it was going to affect my little sisters. He said I was ruining my life.

The words hurt, but the pain was eased a little when I spoke to Mom later.

"I'm so glad you did not answer his call," she said, her voice as loving and kind as ever. "He wasn't in a good state of mind."

From that point on, my relationship with Pops was nearly all hornets and garter snakes. It seemed to me that he was realizing that he was losing control of me. He'd text verses reminding me to "honor thy father and mother," and every conversation we had just heaped more guilt on me, leaving fear gripping my throat even tighter. Often he would text me and apologize, but the messages were often followed up by more words condemning our actions or calling us out. His apologies felt insincere and invalid. Hardly a day would go by without some barbed message from him—either directly or from one of my siblings—and it got so that I didn't want to talk to him anymore.

Days after I'd had my nose pierced, he asked me to have a call with him and Mom. I told him no and put my feelings down in a text.

Honestly, I don't really feel like talking when I feel like there might be a chance I'm just going to be verbally abused, manipulated, and emotionally hurt. It makes me want to shy away from any type of conversation . . . I don't want our relationship to be this way, Daddy. And I know we aren't always going to agree on everything. But we won't want to ask for counsel if we feel like we aren't going to be heard. And you are only going to attack us and insist that your view is the way we should see things too. We wouldn't ask you to agree, but only to listen . . . I love you, Daddy, and believe me, it hurts my heart to know that there would be any kind of disagreement, but life isn't a cookie cutter, there will be differences. I just want to have good relationships with you and Mama and our siblings, even if we aren't on the same page with things. We know you still have littles in the house and that creates a different dynamic that you have to look out for them. But we don't want to feel like you have to turn against us, turn us against each other either . . . I know you will have to talk with them about differences and convictions like the nose ring thing. But I do feel you have a lot of control over how they view us . . . We love y'all and all of our siblings and family and families and seek to honor the Lord and live in right relationship with him and fellow believers. We also recognize that differences can be hard for you too, Daddy. We want to be considerate of that, too. And show that despite our differences, we still love and respect you . . . Love you, Daddy.

I don't know what I thought would happen. I guess I'd hoped that Pops would give a genuine apology, not one that he followed up with attacks or justifications. Maybe he'd let me explain to him about the pants and the nose ring and actually try to see things from our perspective. Maybe, from this low point, we might even be able to finally form a relationship where he saw me as an adult, a mama of my own, not a kid to be disciplined and controlled.

But none of that happened.

Pops dug in.

He hated the hunk of metal in my nose. He despised how I was dressing in ways that put sexual thoughts in guys' minds. Instead of his Sweet Jilly Muffin, I was now a threat to the rest of his children, and a threat to his authority.

For me, the hornets buzzed louder. The snakes came closer.

Fear and guilt. Guilt and fear. At times it was almost hard to breathe.

———⚬⚬⚬———

CHAPTER EIGHT

Pushed Aside

2017 ended badly.

2018 started worse.

We received news from the missionary organization that we'd been hoping to serve with. They'd been waiting almost a year for us to provide some kind of legal confirmation that we were no longer bound by the contract that I'd signed the day before my wedding day. Despite us asking Pops, Chad, and the network repeatedly—either for a release or at least a full copy of the contract itself—we still had nothing to show them other than the typed-up bullet points which Chad had shared telling us the contract ran "for five years" until June 2019, and the partial contract pages from Pops that didn't give us all the information we needed. We'd lost the Panama job, and they'd kept us on their reserve list for as long as they could, but time had run out. If we ever did get free and wanted to serve with them, we'd have to reapply and go through the process again, which would take years.

We were devastated. The mission field had been the one place where I felt free, and I had been so sure that we were called to serve there. We'd already waited a year, and with Pops refusing to cooperate, we would have to wait another year and a half before we could even think about getting out of the contract and serving with the mission organization, *if* they'd have us again. Neither Derick nor I felt able to put our lives on hold for that long.

I was upset. A while later I finally told my mom about losing the job, and eventually Pops found out. We were together one evening when he brought it up.

"You should have told me," he said. "I'm sure we could have worked something out."

I bit my lip so hard I thought I might draw blood.

"No, Pops," said Derick. "That's not the point. You aren't entitled to know what's going on in our lives. What would have been most helpful would have been to stick up for us to TLC, explain everything to them and get us released from the contract."

Around the same time, he texted us, finally giving us just a small but crucial piece of the puzzle—the date when the contract expired.

It wasn't 2019 after all. It was June 2018.

We were both so shocked and upset. Our future had been affected yet again by a lack of transparency, by Pops operating on a need-to-know basis. If we'd known about the expiration date for the contract, then maybe the missions organization would have held on just a little longer. If Pops had been transparent with us earlier, then maybe we might have been able to get back on the mission field without delay. And maybe if we'd told Pops about everything that had been going on with the IMB earlier, then he would have helped sooner, but neither of us had wanted to give him that level of control over our lives, or open the possibility of him making contact with the IMB directly and trying to use his influence to persuade them to bend the rules for us. We wanted to stand on our own two feet.

For a while we considered making contact with the organization again to see if this new information changed anything, but we decided against it. We still didn't have factual proof or all the information—no contract in hand, just a text message. Derick had taken the LSAT and applied to law school, and he'd just heard that he'd been accepted. The way we saw it, a little legal training might be beneficial for us both in the future. The lawsuit that my sisters and I initiated against the people who had released the investigation was still in the early stages. *In Touch* had filed a successful motion to be dismissed from the lawsuit, and we were discovering that as "public figures" we weren't allowed as much protection as "private figures," though we still hoped to maybe prove later the intentional mishandling of juvenile records which could bring them back into the suit down the road. The city and county and their defendants were filing appeals on parts of their suits, but things were still rolling there, slowly but surely.

We tried to put the ending of our IMB plans behind us, but after Easter things flared up again. Derick had been making comments on Twitter, speaking his mind about various topics and making a few enemies. It earned him a quiet conversation with Pops and a warning. "Be careful," he said. "If you've got problems, come to me."

Neither of us felt much like taking him up on his offer at first. We had tried that before and it didn't go over well. So instead, we did what we could to swallow our frustration and tried to avoid doing anything else that would inflame Pops. But when the problems continued, we thought it best to not just sweep them under the rug and continue pretending. We decided to take Pop's advice about coming to him with our problems, but not in person this time. Based on our recent history, and wanting a little buffer, we decided to put our thoughts down in a letter.

We took days working on it. We tried hard to make sure that it was clear and free from too much emotion. We just wanted to list everything that had troubled us, to make sure that Mom and Pops had the best chance possible of understanding where we were at and what we were feeling.

What started out as a page or two quickly expanded. We added paragraph after paragraph of things we really wanted to get resolved. It was a long, long letter—twenty-seven pages in total—and by the time we'd finished it we were worn out. Instead of sleeping on it or checking it over, we decided to send it just as it was. Besides, we were away on a trip to Texas as a family with Derick's ministry program, so it seemed like the perfect opportunity to have a little extra physical distance between us too.

We were relieved and somewhat confused when Pops emailed back a short reply, not answering the questions we'd asked, but apologizing for "all of the ways that my actions & controlling spirit & lack of sensitivity & lack of communication have hurt you and Jill." He thanked us for bringing it to his attention, asked for prayer and begged our forgiveness, adding that he loved us very much.

Then, just as summer began, we came home one day to a letter. And that's when everything finally fell apart.

* * *

It was from the IRS, so to me, it was just another letter from the government that was hard to understand and easy to ignore. Ever since I could remember, Pops' CPA had filed my taxes for me, and for both Derick and I together the first couple years of marriage until we got someone else to do our taxes, and so my initial instincts were to send it on to him. Derick thought otherwise. His degree from OSU was in accounting, and he'd spent a year and a half working in the tax department at Walmart HQ, so he studied the letter carefully.

"What is it?" I asked.

"I don't know yet. But I don't like it."

In the days that followed, Derick tackled the letter like he was a forensic accountant. We emailed Pops' CPA, nonchalantly asking for copies of all my tax records since I'd become an adult. Once we had those, Derick created spreadsheets, looked back over old tax returns, and did what he could to decode the mystery.

Finally, he figured it out and sat me down to explain it all.

"Remember the eighty thousand dollars that Pops paid you?"

"Yeah."

"I think your dad's accountant has been telling the IRS that you've been receiving income from the show that you haven't actually been paid."

"What about the eighty thousand dollars? Doesn't that cover it?"

"Nope. As far as I can tell, over the last ten years, income from Mad Family Inc. that you've declared to the IRS is way higher than that."

"How much?"

Derick checked his spreadsheet again. "About a hundred and thirty thousand dollars more."

We followed up with Pops' CPA via email, asking him to help explain two things—how Pops had reached the eighty-thousand-dollar figure in the first place, and why there was such a vast difference between that and what had been declared on our returns. The fact that we had waited years to see a copy of the contract, and were still waiting, meant that neither of us held out much hope for a quick or detailed reply.

His response did come soon, though I really think the CPA was in the dark on a lot of it, because his answers seemed to show that he thought we'd been aware of more than we actually were.

Pops wasn't offering too much help, either. Though he did dodge the question and gave us some unsolicited advice:

"It's important not to live off your life savings but to reinvest it," he said. "Jason bought a house and fixed it up, and now is reselling it. You guys could do the same. Instead of paying rent, buy a house and fix it up, that would save you rent and multiply your savings."

He also said that he noticed within us a "spirit of ungratefulness." It seemed clear to me that he didn't like us questioning his financial decisions. Typically, he'd have been a little smoother, trying to win us over. But now he sounded like he'd had enough, like we'd exhausted his patience and he couldn't wait for the emails to end and for us to stop asking questions so he could move on. Derick tactfully tried to explain that if we in fact had income, we would like to tithe on it. He said he had already paid the taxes and tithed our portion. Pops explained that if we wanted to tithe on our income, then he would have to kick some families to whom he was giving free rent out of their homes. What we wanted most was transparency and to figure out why I hadn't been paid what had been reported to the government.

Pops' reply contained a question of his own.

"Derick. What amount do you feel like you and Jill are owed?"

It wasn't meant to be a question that invited an answer. It seemed like it was a challenge. As the emails between us and Pops continued, it felt like he was daring us to say a number, daring us to show him disrespect. It wasn't like him to be so harsh, and I wasn't used to feeling such coldness coming off him. I loved Pops and hated the conflict, so part of me just wanted to give up. I wondered if this was all even worth the fight. I just wished we could handle this civilly and without things getting so heated.

The Fourth of July was just around the corner, and for the first time ever Derick and I agreed not to join in the annual celebrations at a friend's house where I knew my parents would be in attendance. It felt like a big decision, and we needed to put a little space between us. I'd hoped that if we could just give some space and let things cool down a little, things might improve.

A period of space wasn't my only idea. First, I asked Mom and Pops whether they'd be willing to meet with a mediator to help us talk through some of our issues in a constructive way. They agreed, and even said they'd be happy for us to pick the mediator and set the time. I appreciated that and hoped that after a couple of weeks we'd be able to all sit together and work things out.

My plan hit a hurdle early on. I had asked my church to recommend some people to facilitate the meeting, and they'd given me three names of people who could sit with all of us and mediate. Finding a time that they could all make work was difficult, so it got narrowed to just two of the three. Then Derick started law school in August, which added more pressure to our lives and schedule. Finally, we settled on a date in the first week of October, but at the last minute the other mediator had to drop out, leaving just one.

I had gone three months without seeing Pops or going over to the Big House at all. It was strange, and I felt estranged from the family, but it was easier to stay away rather than spend time with everyone and try to pretend like everything was just fine.

I was nervous when we arrived at the church for our meeting. We were early, and talked briefly with a friend of Derick's from the school of ministry who was waiting outside. She had tattoos and a nose piercing, but I also knew she was a big fan of the show. When the mediator arrived, we went inside and waited for Mom and Pops.

Pops had a wide smile when he walked through the door. As we exchanged awkward greetings and hugs, Pops held out his phone.

"Look at this," he said.

Derick, the mediator, and I moved in to look as Pops pressed play on a video he'd just recorded. It was the girl from outside, and her smile was even bigger than Pops'. She was saying how her life before had been so full of sin, but watching the show had helped her change. She'd started wearing skirts and signed up for the school of ministry so that she could be near the Duggars. And now, to actually be meeting Pops and Mom in person, it was such a great day for her.

"Isn't that great?" Pops said, eyes wide and sparkling as he looked at each of us. "She's so sweet."

It was nothing new. Ever since he got a smartphone Pops had

been taking videos of anyone he'd met who complimented him on the show and how it had made a positive impact on their lives, then he'd share it with the rest of the family on the group text. To him, it was a way of encouraging people, a reminder of what the ministry was all about. In the past I would probably have agreed. But this time it just stung, watching him pour out praise on the girl with the tattoos and the nose ring. How could he have such a problem with me wearing pants and having my nose pierced, yet appear to overlook whatever this girl had done to her body?

I shook it off and tried to focus.

Derick and I had come prepared, and I checked the note on my phone for the things we wanted to discuss.

That it's not sinful for a woman who fears the Lord to wear pants, have a nose ring, or cut her hair.

That Pops wasn't just disorganized or forgetful when he had me sign the contract without seeing it. It was a deliberate deception.

We want Pops to be fully transparent by finally sharing the 2014 contract with us and telling us about any other agreements that affect us.

Pops can make things right by paying us the full amount that his accountant has reported on my tax returns. Total $130,249.98.

When Derick and I had been talking in the days and weeks leading up to this meeting, those four points had seemed like the most basic things we wanted to agree on. They'd seemed reasonable and possible at the time, and I'd let myself imagine how good it would feel to have reached a resolution on them all. But sitting in the room, with the mediator introducing himself and thanking us all for being there and Pops looking confident and strong and like nothing in the world could ever touch him, I felt different.

So when the mediator invited me to go first, I put the four points out of my mind and just tried to say what I thought would help.

"I'm sorry it took so long for this meeting to happen," I said. My voice was shaking a little, and I could feel the breath stutter in my lungs. "There have been some very hurtful things that have happened, and so we wanted to sort it all out. To have a good discussion together. We love y'all and I know we all hope to be able to restore family relationships very soon."

In the time I'd spoken, Pops' body language had shifted. He wasn't smiling from the video and the girl outside anymore. Instead, he was sitting very still, lips tight, eyes locked in a scowl that had been sculpted out of rock.

"That letter you guys sent us." He stopped, like he was lost and didn't know where to go. He looked at Mom. She looked at me.

There was no scowl on her face, no folded arms. Just a look of pain. The pain of a mama torn by her baby.

"It was the most disrespectful thing I've ever read."

Her voice was soft, but her words hit me harder than anything she'd ever said to me.

I knew she was right, that she was speaking the truth. I didn't know exactly *how* I'd messed up, but I knew that I had. I'd hurt her and Pops, and that was never my intention.

I heard Derick try to explain that we never meant for the letter to be taken that way. I looked at Pops. He was still scowling.

"I'm sorry," I said. "We love y'all and could've used more care. We wrote the letter together and had hoped it would help explain our feelings, but I know we kept adding to it and then we were tired and just figured we had better go ahead send it along . . ."

My voice trailed off as I tried to find the right words. But Pops wasn't listening to me. He had his own list of things he wanted to talk about.

"You sent me a text message, Jill. You said I was verbally abusing you. I was so offended by that, too. You know in your heart that's not right. Are you going to apologize for that?"

I was nervous now. I remembered the message, remembered sending it in the hope that it might wake Pops up to how bad I felt things had gotten, to maybe make him give us a little space and let things calm down. I'd written about not wanting to be verbally abused, which was exactly how I'd felt at the time. I'd felt it in El Salvador as well. I wasn't sure that I could apologize for that. I glanced at Derick as I remained speechless.

Pops must have sensed what I was thinking, because he suddenly stood up. "You're not going to apologize? Really?"

His voice was loud, and there was an edge to it that I'd rarely heard. The moderator looked pale and was stuck on mute. Derick tensed, and I could feel him getting ready to step in. I squeezed his hand, hoping he'd get the message.

Hold back.

Please be quiet.

Do not let this get any worse than it already is.

We were sitting in a horseshoe formation, the moderator in the middle, with the Dillards and Duggars facing each other from opposite couches, open space between us. Pops took a step toward me, closing the gap.

It wasn't a gesture of reconciliation.

It was an act of aggression.

He towered over me, his whole body fueled with anger. My face flushed red. My eyes filled with tears.

Then there was a long, awful silence that I wanted to fill but just couldn't yet.

Derick's hand was shaking in mine, and I squeezed as hard as I ever had, desperate for him to hold his tongue.

"You know why you're crying, don't you? Your conscience is talking to you. That's why."

Pops' voice was so loud in my ears. His words were like blows. I instinctively tried to protect myself and block him out. I curled up on my seat, trying to find safety in some kind of fetal position.

"You're guilty!" Pops was yelling, stabbing a finger at me, standing right over me.

Mom started crying.

Derick tried to speak, but I pulled him back.

"You want to know why I'm crying?" My voice was cracked, my eyes burning. "It's that you think I'm some kind of horrible person just because I wear pants and have a nose ring, and yet you see that girl outside and praise her. That's why I'm crying, Daddy. I'm evolving and changing, just like that girl out there, but you can't see it. You treat me like I'm a prodigal who's turned her back on you. You treat me worse than you treat my pedophile brother."

Pops looked stunned. "Well . . . ," he stammered. I wondered whether he was about to agree with me, to confirm that in his mind my sins of disobedience really were as bad as what Josh had been doing.

But finally, the moderator spoke up. "I think we should take a break."

* * *

The mediation meeting lasted three hours. Three hours of raised voices, flowing tears from my mother and me, and not much in the way of resolution. We didn't even get to ask about the money situation or some of the other things we'd hoped to discuss. By the time it was over, my head was pounding, my heart felt like it had been beaten raw. It was almost impossible to concentrate, but I heard clearly what the mediator said to Derick and me once Mom and Pops left.

"You need professional help."

We agreed and began searching for a therapist right away. We found someone quickly—we'll call him Mr. Ray McIntosh—a silver-haired licensed Christian therapist who had a space for us in his calendar. Derick was all in from the moment we made our initial appointment, but I had some baggage to work through.

"A therapist is just someone you're paying to be your friend." I'd heard it said often when I was growing up, and it was on repeat in my head. So too was Pops warning us repeatedly about talking to people outside the family about anything to do with either the show or the family. "They might not understand. And they might not be in line with IBLP teachings." It was the old umbrella of protection again, making me terrified of thinking for myself.

Like the fallout of a nuclear blast, I was beginning to hate the way the IBLP umbrella principle continued to affect me. I hated how much of a hold it still had on my life, even though I'd tried to tackle it so many times before. I hated the fact that I was still having to deal with it. I wished I could sort things out and I was tired of the toll it was taking on me emotionally. I wanted help, but I was scared to be one of *those* people, the kind who looked to the world to solve their problems instead of to God.

It wasn't all bad. Just when things were at their bleakest, Samuel was due for his eighteen-month checkup—the one that would determine whether he had sustained any long-term brain damage at birth. The results, according to the neurologist, were conclusive: there was no lasting sign at all of any brain damage from the birth. It was a rare piece of good news, and it left me ecstatic for days.

By the time we walked into our first therapy session, I was ready to talk. The words tumbling out of us both, while our therapist sat and listened, occasionally steering us back on course.

At the end of the session, Ray delivered his verdict. "I've tried to do those group mediation sessions before and they're very hard to do. It's not easy to keep a handle on the room, and it can easily turn into a shouting match."

"Yeah," I said, my mind flashing back to me curled up on the chair while Pops jabbed a finger in time with his shouting and our first mediator just sat silent and stunned.

"I would recommend that you guys see a therapist, whether it's me or somebody else, for a few sessions. Your parents can see someone else as well, and when you're ready you could sign something to allow the two therapists to talk and help be the go-between for a while. Then maybe you can eventually meet together with your parents . . . but I don't know if I'd recommend that."

It sounded good and we shared the plan with Mom and Pops. To their credit, they contacted the other therapist that Mr. McIntosh had recommended and had a session together. But the more time we spent in therapy ourselves, the more it became clear to us that we were a long, long way from being able to put in place the solutions that would fix our relationship with my parents. First, we had to understand how deep our wounds went and how much healing was needed.

People were starting to notice that something was up. Bloggers and tabloids and people on social media had spotted that Derick and I hadn't appeared in any photos posted by the family for months. The longer we stayed hidden, the more the rumors spread. It didn't help that TLC never aired our exit interviews and there was no announcement of us leaving. We had just disappeared from the show without any of the exit interview footage being used, so people speculated. Some people said we'd been fired from the show. Others said it was all because of Derick's Twitter comments. One thread I saw was all about how Derick had obviously ordered me to start wearing pants because Jinger had gotten so much attention for it and Derick was just desperate to be noticed.

It was all ridiculous, and for Derick and me it was easy enough to ignore. For Pops, it was another matter. Anything that damaged the show damaged him, so he seemed anxious to get back to the mediation, to make things right between us all and have us back over to the Big House again, just like old times.

"You can't put a timeline on healing," said our therapist when we asked him how long it was going to take before we were ready to meet with Mom and Pops again. "You're just going to have to tell them that at this point we don't know when you'll be ready. I think we need to focus your energies on your own healing right now."

It was good advice, the kind that makes you exhale with relief. Finally, we had someone on our side. And after all those years of having to fit in with whatever schedule worked for the show, I could say no. I could follow my own timetable.

Even in just a few sessions, Ray had helped us see how to communicate more effectively with Pops. We realized that the long letter we'd written in the summer had been all kinds of wrong. We'd put way too many accusations in it and we hadn't owned how we felt about it. There was no way for Pops to read it and not feel offended.

So, when I sent a message to Pops and Mom about when we'd be ready to meet again, I took our therapist's advice. I explained that we felt like we needed some time to work on ourselves, apologized for the fact that everything was taking longer than we'd hoped again, and thanked them for being willing to work on this with us.

It was good to feel empowered like this, and I was fine with waiting as long as it took for Derick and me to heal. But there was one issue that we couldn't put on hold indefinitely—money.

Back when Derick had enrolled at Oklahoma State University as a teenager, his mom and dad had given him some great advice: apply for every grant, every scholarship possible. He did exactly what they said and sent out almost a hundred letters, applications and essays to various boards and nonprofits and foundations that he had a chance of receiving financial aid from. Then they started rolling in, including $20,000 from OSU, nearly $10,000 from the Buck Foundation, and $1,000 from the local Walmart Neighborhood Market.

He ended up getting almost half his costs covered, saving himself tens of thousands of dollars over the course of his degree.

Naturally, when he enrolled in law school over a decade later, Derick took the same approach. With two kids under four at home, and a wife who wasn't working, money was even tighter than it had been before. He needed all the grants he could get, so he began applying.

It didn't take long for him to realize that all the money that Pops' accountant had declared on my tax returns made it look like we had way more cash than we actually did. It didn't matter that we'd never actually been paid the $132,249.98 which had been declared. As far as these trusts and foundations were concerned, our tax returns told the story that we didn't need much financial help. While that was frustrating, that wasn't even our biggest worry. We worried more about what we still didn't know about our finances, the contract, and previous taxes with Pops.

We had been pushing Pops to pay us the bare minimum ever since the summer, and we had hoped to reach an agreement in the mediation session, but we hadn't even discussed it. There had been more follow-up emails and texts. We'd got an email from him a couple weeks later, and as I read the opening lines, I felt genuinely surprised:

> *Jill & Derick,*
> *We love you both and want to see our differences resolved.*
> *I have been praying and fasting about all of this.*
> *I need to share my heart with you . . .*
> *I have made some bad decisions along life's way, and have hurt you all. I am sorry about that.*

I was wrong for things I have said and done, and I pray you will please forgive me.

It was a good start. Maybe he'd had a change of heart and was actually going to reconcile with us after all.

But the further I read, the worse I felt.

Yes, we allotted, at different times, amounts to our children, for tax purposes, because each one of our children were benefiting from having all of their needs met (food, clothing, shelter, utilities, music lessons, education, travel, instruments, vehicles, phones, medical insurance, medical bills, etc.).

Here are some low numbers of what was approximately spent on Jill in the last few years:

Apartment rate rent $750 x 24 months=$18,000

Utilities discounted $600 x 36=$21,600

Midwife education $5,000

Honda Pilot $9,000

Harp $15,000

Furniture $5,000

(If you don't want the furniture, we will buy it back after 4 years of use for $3,000.)

Cell phone @ $50 x 120 months=$6,000

Car insurance $50 per month x 8 years=$4,800

Vehicle fuel (8 years) x $50/month= $4,800

Eating out $100/month with family debit card for 8 years=$9,600

Clothes & Goodwill on family debit cards $1,000 per year x 8 years=$8,000

Eating at home $3 per day x 12 years=$13,140

Gift to Dillard Family Ministries $10,000

(You paid yourself a salary from this, stated there was only $1,200 left when you closed it out, so you must have eventually received it. You can refund this ministry gift, and we will give it to you directly if you want us to.)

$129,940 is just the beginning of Jill's expenses paid by Duggar family over the last several years. Most of this was made and spent on Jill before you two were married.

Also, taking into account many other ways that we have spent money to help you all, for example, installing the AC in your home to El Salvador, the stove, the washing machine, etc.

The total on Jill's tax returns was $130,250.

We would be willing to write a check for $20,000 to settle this once and for all.

Jill, when Mom and I pass on, you are set to receive 1/19th of everything we own that is set up in a trust for you kids.

If you attack us, probably your inheritance will be lowered significantly.

I love you, but I am grieved by the disrespect and the accusations that continue.

I have asked for forgiveness, and I hope that you will also, you have deeply offended your mother and I.

We love you and forgive you for the things you have said & done.

$20,000 is a one-time offer, take it or leave it, please let me know by Monday night, or the amount will be zero.

Love, Daddy Duggar

For all the progress we were making in therapy, for all the desire we had to be on good terms with family and work things out, that email set us back a long way. It felt cold. It felt brutal. It hurt. It seemed Pops wasn't being generous when we thought he was being generous in the past. He was showing us Proverbs 23:1–8 in action.

It was clear that Pops was not only counting the cost of bringing me into the world, he was set on denying our requests. We couldn't just continue the cat-and-mouse game. We were already spent emotionally, and we knew if we didn't move to protect ourselves and remedy the situation, it would only get worse. We couldn't live like that forever, so we decided to act.

In late October, we hired an attorney who sent a formal demand letter to Pops, asking for the 2014 contract as well as copies of the Mad Family Inc. bylaws, minutes, and other details that I, as a shareholder, should have seen already.

Pops went ballistic.

First, he hit the phone. There were texts and voicemails and calls every day, but in none of them did he give the answers we requested. Instead he was calling for us to get things resolved, to move on and work things out. We told him that we wanted to do that too, and that all he had to do was communicate through our attorney, with the information requested.

He didn't.

Then came the next wave, a consolidated effort from several of my siblings. They hit the phones, sending voicemails and texts all day long, each one pleading with us to get this resolved. When that didn't work, some of my siblings started visiting. They'd want to spend hours talking it through, trying to figure out what our problem was and why we weren't doing what Pops wanted. I felt obligated to at least hear them out and show them we cared by listening. I could just about cope with the daytime visits, but when they wanted to stay up until midnight talking with Derick and me, when Derick had law school exams the next day, we finally told them no.

"What? How come you won't talk?" they'd say. "This is way more important than law school."

We could see what was going on. Early in 2017, Pops had started paying small, non-negotiable amounts per episode to those who were filming, both to spouses and siblings. It seemed to me as if they had been brainwashed into thinking that they weren't owed anything, and that the $80,000 payment had been super generous. That they should be nothing but grateful for all the gifts and good favors he was giving them. There were strings attached though—like having to pile on Derick and me when we caused trouble—but it seemed like nearly none of them were willing to question what Pops was doing. They were still so terrified of stirring up dissention among the brethren that they went along with most everything.

Not every visit was designed to apply pressure though. One of my siblings came alone and told us what was really going on.

"Pops is telling everyone that if we don't stand against you both on this, then we're standing against him. He said none of us can be neutral here, and that this affects all of us. He says we might all be sued as a result of what you're doing."

When my sibling left, I cried. It was one thing for Pops to be angry at Derick and me, but how could he justify bringing his other children into it like this? How could he mislead them into thinking they might be sued, when he knew full well it was the Mad Family Inc. corporation we were dealing with, not our siblings? It made me sad for him. It made me scared for them.

Our attorney told us to stay calm and ride it out, calmly repeating our demands when Pops refused to cooperate. For him it was standard lawyer stuff, but for me, it was a nightmare.

I wasn't coping so well. I'd feel a fear-spiked adrenaline rush kick in every time my phone screen lit up with a Duggar family name. Each knock on the door felt like we were back in El Salvador with armed gangs prowling around.

One day, around the end of November, another one of my siblings paid us a visit. For once there was no conversation to be had.

"Here," they said, holding out a piece of paper. "Pops says you've got twenty-four hours."

Derick and I studied the page after my sibling left. Pops was still trying to make a deal with us outside of our formal request for just the Mad Family documents and contract. It was the same deal we'd seen before. He wanted to pay us $20,000 that day and have us sign an NDA that would keep us from talking about any of it. We had no intention of signing it.

Our attorney maintained our requests as he continued the discussions with Pops and his CPA over email. As the deadline for handing over the documents grew closer, we started talking about the next step—possibly obtaining a court order to gain the release of the documents we were requesting.

"Will it work?" I asked Derick. "Do you think he will give us what we are asking for?"

"Yeah. I don't think he will let it get to that point."

It was late and the boys were asleep and I was feeling cold. But my shivering was nothing to do with the temperature. It was raw fear.

"How do you know?"

"Because what we're asking for is perfectly reasonable. Because we have a right to them and it makes sense to anyone who looks at it objectively, including a judge or jury." Derick exhaled. "Because Pops values the show and wouldn't want all of this to be public and jeopardize the show."

For months I'd been trying to hold in all the fear and sorrow. There was nobody I could talk to about it, apart from our therapist, and at times those therapy sessions were like jumping into a frozen lake. We'd be discussing some of the recent difficulties with Pops and exploring how it related to parts of my upbringing, and all the blood would be rushing in my ears. My thoughts would spiral so much that I'd mainly remember those sessions with Ray like a dream.

I could feel myself unraveling. All my edges were frayed. Throughout my whole life I'd had my family around me. And IBLP had preached the importance of the immediate core family relationships always being prioritized above relationships with others, causing some to still define them as immediate and prioritize them above all relationships well into marriage. Now most of them were against me. I wasn't built for this. I'd experienced stress and trauma before—some of it caused by individuals in my family—but I'd always been able to count on the rest for support. They had been my gravity, the force that I never had to question and could always rely upon. But now it felt like they were gone. Some were still there, but it was different and more distant than before. They didn't know how to handle it either. Despite having my own wonderful family of four, there was a part of me that felt alone. I had no frame of reference for dealing with that.

I woke up one night to the sound of our storm door opening. Someone started hammering on the door. It was 12:15 a.m.

My heart was instantly hammering in my chest. I was freaking out, reaching for Derick. He was groggy at first, but when the doorbell rang, he shot up out of bed.

"Wait!" I hissed as he headed out of the room.

"Who is it? Are they seriously breaking in?"

I was at the window. I couldn't see who was out there, but there was a car out on the street. A car that I recognized.

"It's Mom's car," I said. "And . . ."

Whoever had been hammering and knocking on the door gave up, turned around and walked back to the car. It was Mom. She'd never done anything like that before—nobody in my family had—and I stared out the window at her, frozen.

I watched her go.

The adrenaline took hours to leak from my body.

Neither of us could figure out why she'd come, but a long fifteen minutes later, after she'd been gone awhile and we were climbing back into bed, unable to sleep, we got a text:

Jill & Derick,
We love you all.
I took the discovery contract in its entirety to your house late last night.
I apologize for going by so late.
I left it in between your screen door and front door. 🖤
—Mom

Sure enough, when we opened the door in the morning, there was an envelope wedged at the base of the storm door. Inside was a copy of the contract from 2014. All thirty pages of it. They hadn't worked it out through our attorney like we'd requested, but we were glad to have it in hand now. And a part of me felt like them bringing it over may have been a last-minute emotional decision which may not have happened if they'd waited.

We spent most of the morning studying the contract. Derick had to translate some of the legal language for me, but there was plenty in it that I didn't need any help with.

Like part three, titled "Compensation."

It stated that for each half hour episode, Mad Family Inc. would be paid $50,000, and for each one-hour episode $65,000, with the numbers rising to $58,000 and $73,000 if the show hit a fourth season.

Pops later determined somehow that each child would receive 3 percent on their tax return each year. However, even this was a phantom payment, seemingly just reported on paper for tax purposes with no apparent intention to actually pay out this amount. We would later be told that this previously reported income was an investment or inheritance that we could only have access to upon my parents' death.

We did the numbers. Over the years there had been well over three hundred shows, for which we estimated that TLC had paid Mad Family Inc. over $8,000,000 total. Our wedding alone had netted well over $100,000 for Pops, and Israel's birth had been the focus of two special episodes, earning Pops another six-figure sum. Yet when we'd asked him to cover our $10,000 deductible and out-of-pocket expenses from the hospital stay, he'd pushed back.

Over the years Pops had bought more and more properties, and his fleet of private aircraft now contained multiple airplanes, including one with ten seats. There was no denying that he was a generous man who had helped a lot of people, but it was also true that he'd grown rich off the show and had fought hard to keep that under wraps.

It was hard to face the reality that my own father had seemingly tricked me on the day of my wedding rehearsal into signing such a document.

While we were emailing our attorney about the contract, one of my siblings called me. They sounded excited and wanted me to know that they had talked with Pops and that he was suddenly ready to pay the $130,000. They explained that he had some conditions—like wanting to handle it in house, without our attorney, and have us sign an NDA. I thanked my sibling for their thoughtfulness but reminded them that we had already tried working things out multiple times with Pops without an attorney, and that our only current request via our attorney was still not fully met as we were still lacking the other Mad Family documents. I told them that at this point we would just prefer that Pops communicate with our attorney to get those to us.

It wasn't until January that things were finally resolved. We got some, but not all, of the Mad family documents since they were missing some, and our attorney had spent weeks going back and forth negotiating the final settlement. We didn't sign an NDA or anything of that nature. And though we hadn't asked for what we felt was the true value of what I had provided to the show, at least it would help me recover what was owed to me that had previously been reported on my taxes, plus cover attorney fees, as well as buy me out of my shares and future profits of Mad Family Inc.

Once I signed, I drove to our attorney's office to collect a check— the first of five monthly installments.

I sat in the car, check in my bag, and exhaled.

$175,000 was a lot of money, but I wondered if it would even make a dent in the Mad Family Inc. bank balance. We could have asked for more, I suppose, but we hadn't wanted to be greedy. We just wanted to recover some of what I was owed for the work we had done and maybe also send a message that our contribution to the show, along with my other siblings, should be valued.

So we'd won. We'd got what we wanted. But I wasn't in the mood for celebrating.

I felt like maybe my parents and most of my siblings thought I was greedy, and that Derick and I were horrible people for what we'd done to the family. Maybe they were right.

I never knew that victory could feel so hollow or so overwhelmingly sad.

———∞∞∞———

CHAPTER NINE

Real. Not Fake

I knew nothing about cocktails, but even from the first sweet sip I could tell that the piña colada was a good one. It was September 2020, a late summer date night for Derick and me, and everything always tasted better when it was just the two of us, sitting side by side in a booth, sharing stories about the boys, sketching future plans like we had on the back porch of our house in El Salvador. But this night, just like this piña colada, was special. It felt like a night to celebrate.

Israel had just started school. Sending your firstborn off on day one is a big enough milestone for every parent, but for me, it felt even more significant. Homeschooling was at the very heart of what IBLP stood for, and they loved quoting Proverbs 22:6 ("Train up a child in the way he should go: and when he is old, he will not depart from it"). It was a nonnegotiable for any true IBLP member, and it was one of the things that first attracted my parents to Mr. Gothard's

Date night, September 2020

teaching. And their homeschooling conferences, resources, and training continued to be a big part of the IBLP business model. As a result, not one of my siblings or any of their children had been sent to a public school. I'd been brought up to view the public school system as dangerous and ungodly, and to view anyone who didn't choose to homeschool their kids as an uninformed or risky parent.

Our decision to enroll Israel in public school represented a significant step on my own journey out from IBLP—an organization that I was finally able to see clearly. It was a cult, thriving on a culture of fear and manipulation. Derick—who was a perfect example of how a godly man can thrive in public school—helped challenge my thinking. The more we had talked and prayed about sending

Israel to public school, the clearer the issue became for me: IBLP had put a lot more energy into teaching me to fear the world beyond its doors than it had put into teaching me to trust God and discern for myself how to reach a good and wise decision on any given issue.

I guess that was why I didn't move the piña colada out of the shot when Derick took a photo of us at the end of the meal. I was going to. When he reached for his phone, I reached out a hand to move the half-empty glass, but then I stopped. Derick had drunk a beer and I'd had my cocktail. It was a special kid-free date time, just the two of us. So, I left it where it was on the table. In the shot. There for everyone to see when I posted the photo later on. I didn't want to be fake. I wanted to be real.

The whole piña colada picture got some people upset. The story—such as it was—got picked up by *People* magazine and others, but it wasn't anything like the nose ring or the time I started wearing pants. It must have triggered one of Pops' Google alerts, but there was no communication from him. I guess he had gotten the hint a few months earlier when he read online that Derick had been seen drinking a beer. Pops had made contact soon after and offered to send Derick to the same rehab facility Josh had been to, in the hope of curing Derick's clearly raging alcoholism. Since he'd never been drunk or ever had more than two beers in any one sitting, Derick declined.

My desire to be genuine had been growing steadily within me for a long time. Two months had passed since I'd walked out of the attorney's office with the first check for the money declared to the IRS. Pops had left me in no doubt that by pushing him to pay the money we believed we were owed, I wouldn't just be stepping

away from Mad Family Inc. I would be placing a large barrier between me and the rest of the Duggar family, and giving Pops control
of the narrative my siblings would likely hear. It was daunting, but
I knew that Derick and I had made the right decision. And in the
year and a half that followed, my journey toward acknowledging
and embracing my real self had gathered pace.

At first, things were tough. But for every moment where I felt a
sense of relief at getting out from Pops' control, there were a dozen
more times when the fear and the guilt felt just as dangerous and
painful as they had ever been. We'd left the show, we'd cut the rope
that bound us tight to the family, so by rights we should have felt at
liberty to make new, deep friendships with people. But all I felt was
worried. There were days when I felt more alone than ever. I'd recently read the book *Boundaries* by Dr. Henry Cloud and Dr. John
Townsend and found it very helpful, validating, and encouraging.

Things had gotten worse in April 2019 when Pops sent me a text
that included the words "please don't come over when I am not
at home." We had already started to feel uncomfortable hanging
out at the Big House—sometimes it felt like we'd have to get the
courage up before hanging out with some of my family members
in any setting. Even Derick was starting to feel the pressure, which
manifested itself in the form of an all-out panic attack around Easter
time. Being effectively banned from the Big House felt like a reac-
tionary and cruel blow.

Yet in the middle of those dark times, one thing we never failed
to be grateful for was the chance to continue seeing Ray for counseling every week. He was a voice of calm in the storm, a steady,
unchanging presence when everything else was in a state of decay.

Thanks to him I learned a lot about myself, especially when it came to the issue of trusting people. Pops had always warned us about talking to people outside the family—and even advising us against speaking to those inside the family at times—so I'd always found it difficult to be honest with people about things I was struggling with. I was hardwired to be wary, and after everything that happened with *In Touch* magazine and the story of Josh's abuse, I found it almost impossible to open up to people.

"Have you heard of the word 'attunement'?" Ray asked us one session. Derick and I both looked blank, so he went on to explain about the importance of couples learning to communicate with each other on a deep, emotional level—becoming *attuned*. Instinctively I liked it, and Derick and I added the word to our vocabulary. We needed it. Somehow, throughout all the chaos around the show and with my family, we'd stayed strong together. We'd been united through all the turmoil, but we still needed help. By introducing this idea of us being attuned to each other, Ray helped us to communicate on a deeper level than we'd been on before.

He knew how to challenge us, encouraging us to talk with others. He advised us to pick a small circle of close friends who we trusted and start talking with them. He also gave us better tools to help us open the lines of communication with my family.

For our homework one week he said we should draw a target. "Write the names of friends and family inside different rings of the target with the middle being your closest, most trusted relationships, to the widest being the more distant ones. This exercise will help you visualize your relationships, and it's okay if it takes a while to figure out. Those relationships will change at different points in your life, and that's okay too."

It was harder than I thought, and I almost felt guilty not putting all of my family in the inner circle. But it brought clarity and was a helpful, practical step for us as a couple to verbalize and decide which relationships we felt safest in and in which ones we needed healthier boundaries.

"Take a risk," Ray told us when we discussed next week's exercise. He advised us to cultivate close friendships and talk with some of my siblings about problems we'd faced. "If you can share a little bit more about the things you're struggling with, it gives them permission to do likewise."

It wasn't easy. After so many years of being warned not to "stir up contention among the brethren," I was preprogrammed to keep my thoughts to myself. But as soon as I opened up for the first time—saying yes to one of my brothers when he told me he liked a girl and asked if he could come over and get my advice on how he should navigate the relationship without Pops taking control—I realized two amazing things. First, that maybe the act of talking about the tough journey that we'd been on could actually be of help to some of the people I loved most and help them avoid some of the same problems we'd faced. Second, when I did talk about it, the sky didn't fall in. And just like drinking a piña colada on a date with my husband, God wasn't angry with me. Muscle memory told me I was sinning, but common sense, long and deep conversations with Derick, as well as my own Bible study, prayer life, and conversations with other Christians told me that I was actually okay. It felt strange, but at twenty-seven years old, I was finally learning to build healthy relationships and have a healthier, less fear driven view of God. And I was realizing it was a whole lot harder to "walk the straight and narrow" Christian road and live with balance than to fall to extremes.

So much of my faith has been shaken over the years, but never more so than when things were so painful with Mom and Pops. It was hard to process everything, hard to pick through everything that I had been taught—both at home and in church—and filter truth from lies. At times it was tempting to throw it all out and run away, but even that terrified me. Growing up I'd heard so many horror stories of people who had become "backsliders" or had "lowered their standards" that just the thought of looking critically at my faith felt dangerous and foreign to me.

Deep down I knew that I didn't want to bail on my faith. I was aware that people had used the Bible to manipulate me and press on the nerve of my guilt in order to make me conform to what they felt was acceptable, but I didn't hold that against God.

God was always there for me. So was Derick. He was strong for me when I needed him, and I couldn't imagine working through something like this without a loving partner by my side.

These Bible verses from Micah 6:6–8 were a comforting reminder of what God expected of me.

"With what shall I come before the LORD,
and bow myself before God on high?
Shall I come before him with burnt offerings,
with calves a year old?
Will the LORD be pleased with thousands of rams,

with ten thousands of rivers of oil?
Shall I give my firstborn for my transgression,
the fruit of my body for the sin of my soul?"
He has told you, O mortal, what is good;
and what does the LORD require of you
but to do justice, and to love kindness,
and to walk humbly with your God?

Talking deeply and honestly felt like a challenge, but it was nothing compared with what had happened that summer. Six months had passed since Pops had given in and paid out that first payment, and I'd not seen him since then. But in June, Grandma Duggar died. She had been a force of nature, and her passing was going to leave a mighty hole in everyone's life, especially Pops. My heart went out to him. For all the disagreement and pain that passed between us—for all the lack of attunement—I felt for him.

When we got the date for Grandma Duggar's funeral, I talked about what I should do with Ray. I had no idea how to navigate it, though I knew for sure that I wanted to go.

"Your dad's going to be hurting," he said. "Seek him out. Go up to him as soon as you can. Don't wait around anxiously for him to come to you. Go straight up and show him that you care."

My throat was dry and my insides were empty as I headed for Tontitown a few days before the funeral. It was only a couple of months after Pops had told me not to go to the Big House when he wasn't there, and it was strange to be feeling so nervous as I pulled down the long gravel drive to the house I had called home for nearly eight years—a house I had helped build. I felt like a visitor, an imposter, and a prodigal all rolled into one. I saw Pops coming out of the house shortly after I parked, and I did what our therapist had suggested and went straight to him.

"I'm so sorry about grandma. I'm sure you must be heartbroken," I said, repeating the words I'd rehearsed in my mind over and over. Then I gave him a hug. I hadn't rehearsed that, but it wasn't anything I could stop. It just felt right.

"Thank you," he said.

For the first time in years, I felt connected to Pops.

Days later, after the funeral, Derick and I were invited back to the Big House. It was nice to be asked, and I'm sure that Sweet Jilly Muffin would have said yes, but her voice wasn't as loud within me anymore. So I said no. I needed to go home and grieve alone.

For Grandma Duggar.

For everything.

I didn't think that hug with Pops would change anything overnight, but I appreciated it all the same. And as summer rolled on, things did begin to shift. Pops still didn't want me going over to the Big House unless he was there, but he did start inviting Derick, the boys, and I along to more family events from time to time, sometimes even pressuring us to show up. Most of the events that we were invited to attend didn't include any cameras, which was fine, though I was tempted to wonder if Pops was partly doing it so that he could post pictures of us and squash the rumors that were circulating online about us splitting from the family. I didn't dwell on it.

I liked spending time with my family, even if it was hard at times. It felt right. I guess it felt right to Pops too, because just before Thanksgiving, the Big House ban was lifted—partially. Mom told us that we were welcome around the Big House anytime, though Pops added a condition, "as long as you are not only coming over when I am not there." It was a subtle change, and I guess he wanted to make sure that we weren't trying to avoid him too much.

Derick and I were still seeing Ray, so there were plenty more opportunities to reflect and try to make sense of the legacy of growing up like I did. With Derick in law school, and our schedule busy, we tried to be intentional about where we got involved in our church and how we continued building new relationships with people. We started volunteering in the kids' ministry on Sunday mornings to be part of the classes our kids were in and make friends with other parents. It was all hands on deck in the chaos of the kids' church, and there really wasn't much opportunity for anyone to ask about my family.

We were in a kids' church meeting one day in November when my phone started blowing up. I could feel it announcing a new text message every minute or so, and when I snuck a look, I saw that they were all around the same theme—something had happened with my family and people were reaching out to tell me they were praying for us.

As soon as our meeting was over, I checked Google and saw that Homeland Security had raided Josh's car lot. Details were scarce and vague, but it was something to do with an investigation. Later that evening, I saw a statement from Pops too, telling the world that nothing was going on and nobody in the family was being investigated. I hated to think it, but the conflicting details led me to believe that he wasn't telling the whole story. I prayed I was wrong.

Once we made it home and got the kids in bed, I talked to one of my siblings who had just been in on things at the Big House.

"That's not all," they said when I asked them about Pops' statement. "He just called a family meeting. Told us Josh was being investigated. He said they took a bunch of hard drives but that it might all be a setup. So he's telling us to pray that this all comes to an end real quick, and reminded us not to make any statements to anyone."

I could imagine the scene. The heavy silence, everyone wondering what was really going on, but nobody asking their questions out loud. All eyes on Pops, standing in the middle, rallying the troops. Mom sitting quiet to the side, looking weary. Like she'd been here too many times already.

For weeks, online rumors danced like a campfire. I stayed away from the gossip, but I was aware that some people were saying that since it was Homeland Security investigating, it must have been an immigration issue. Maybe, I thought. But unlikely.

Mostly I tried to ignore it all. I was grateful for distance between me and the show, grateful that I wouldn't be called upon to do my bit to defend Pops' other baby. But I felt for my siblings. I worried about them feeling the pressure to help Pops out.

Whatever the investigation into Josh was really about, it had kind of died down by the time 2020 began, and especially by the time Covid hit. As the world shut down and governments told people to retreat to their homes, I knew that—figuratively at least—I was done with hiding. I wanted to connect with people, to take a risk and begin to open up.

By late summer of 2020, Covid was still a risk, but I was grateful for the protocols our local public school district had in place to create a healthy environment for the kids to still be able to attend school safely.

So those first few days, as I prayed over Israel and kissed him goodbye and watched him run into kindergarten, I was thankful. Thankful for God's direction and my husband's wisdom and support as we prayerfully made decisions together as a couple that were best for our family. And though I wasn't terrified of sending Israel into public school, I'd be lying if I said I wasn't at least a little nervous.

Maybe that's why the date night piña colada tasted so good. It wasn't just Israel starting a whole new chapter in his life.

I was too.

Being involved in reality TV does strange things to your relationships. It almost denies you the right to choose who is close to you and who isn't—in the way that our therapist challenged us to do with his exercise. There are times when it seems that everyone feels entitled to be in your inner circle, with full access to your life. It also leaves you in a catch-22. After years of having to share almost every aspect of your life with a show, you crave privacy. If you keep quiet and try to hide away, people just spread more lies and rumors about you. If you defend yourself and try to set the record straight, criticized and deemed to be unworthy of privacy.

It's an impossible choice, and there isn't a pain-free option.

For Derick and me, the truth mattered. We've always known

that some people will dislike what we say, do or believe, regardless of the truth. We can't change them, and we have to accept that. But everyone deserves to hear—and to be able to share—the truth.

We both knew that there was more to being real than posting photos on Instagram, and we wanted to go further than laying a few breadcrumbs and hoping that people would figure things out for themselves. We wanted to find a way to put our therapist's advice into practice, so, having thought about it for a while, in October 2020 we decided to shoot a video of the two of us talking about where we were at on a few issues. It was lo-fi, low-key, just Derick and I sitting on the couch, my phone balanced on a stack of books on the coffee table. We set it up like a Q&A and worked through a range of questions. Why did we leave the show? Has there been some distancing with the family and why? Do you see a change in yourselves since therapy? It was a bit hard and a little painful, but it just felt good to be honest with people.

We uploaded it and waited for the reaction.

Viewers left kind, encouraging comments. *People* magazine picked up the story, and we sat down for an interview with them. But the response I was most curious about was Mom and Pops'.

They didn't comment at all.

We were relieved.

On Friday, March 5, 2021, Derick was at home doing some remote learning. Israel was at school and I had been reading to Samuel and working on some other projects when there was a knock on the door. Two men were standing there. One in his late thirties, the other in his mid-forties. Both were wearing dark, collared shirts. Both looked serious.

"Jill Dillard?"

"Yes."

"We're from Homeland Security. Can we ask you some questions about your brother, Josh Duggar?"

I told them I'd want my husband to be able to talk to them as well, but that he was busy right now. So I took their card and promised to call them back to arrange a time.

Three days later they came back as agreed. At first the questions were all about Josh's business, his car lot, who worked for him, and more. I tried my best, but I knew next to nothing about his car lot. I'd driven past it a bunch of times, but I don't think I'd ever visited him there.

"I'm sorry I can't be more helpful," I said.

There was a pause. Then, "What about the abuse incident?"

"I don't want to talk about that," I said.

"Why?"

It was my turn to leave a pause. Time to be real. Not fake.

"I guess two reasons. One, because we have pending litigation with all of that. And two, I just don't want to go there. I'm sorry, but that's just the way it is."

When the *In Touch* story had been published in 2015, my experience with the paparazzi left me feeling traumatized and panicked. It took years for the wounds to begin to heal. I still wasn't able to relax at home without compulsively checking every car parked on the street outside. They kept coming. And they would always try and tie in the earlier abuse to their stories, renewing my trauma. Every year or so, just when I thought I'd gotten used to life without them, they'd be there, waiting outside the house as I came home, following me when I went into town. One time they snapped Derick when he came back from a run, which ended up accompanying the story "Disgraced Derick seems to have a lot of time on his hands after being fired from *Counting On* . . ."

I guess I should have seen it coming. With Josh's investigation not going away, the paparazzi were bound to come back.

It happened a month after Derick and I spoke with the men from Homeland Security. Derick was out at the time and I was at home with the boys. Someone rang the doorbell, and I just assumed it was a delivery.

As soon as I saw him standing on the doorstep, I could tell. The travel-creased clothes, the fake smile that didn't reach his ratty eyes. But no camera that I could see.

"'Ello Jill," he announced, his voice a thick London accent. "I'm from the *Sun*. D'you know you bruvver's about to be arrested? Any comment?"

I was polite but said, "Sorry, no comment," and shut the door. Then I tried to remember how to breathe.

Josh was arrested three days later. From that point on I felt like I'd been hurled straight into a hurricane.

Within hours, one of the Homeland Security guys called to tell me that they were releasing my entire interview to the defense. They were obligated to do it, but I hated it all the same. I was being dragged back into the drama, and I felt powerless to stop it.

A week after the arrest, Derick and I watched Josh's detention hearing online. Derick told me to expect it to last an hour. Instead, it took six. We learned a lot that day about what Josh was being accused of—charges related to him downloading child sexual abuse material. These charges were way more serious than I'd expected, and I was in shock to hear how terrible the crimes he was accused of were. And when the agent from Homeland Security testified about the day they raided Josh's car lot, I was shocked by Josh's initial reactions to the raid. He seemed nervous, even asking, "What is this about? Has someone been downloading child pornography?"

Unsurprisingly TLC canceled the show again, and this time there was no high-profile exclusive interview that could get it back on track. The time of the Duggars being a filming family was officially over.

I tried to keep myself focused on the boys, to not let whatever was happening with Josh trigger me into feeling anxious or panicky again. It wasn't easy, but all those hours Derick and I had spent in therapy helped. I reminded myself often that this wasn't a repeat of the original investigation or the *In Touch* story. It wasn't easy, since there was a media frenzy surrounding every step of Josh's legal process, and the earlier *In Touch* article was brought up in nearly every story. But I could make my own choices. I did not have to get caught up in the family drama anymore.

In August, I found out that wasn't strictly true. Over five years had passed since my sisters and I had started our lawsuit against the City of Springdale, Arkansas; Washington County, Arkansas; Kathy O'Kelley; Ernest Cate; Rick Hoyt; *In Touch* magazine and its parent company Bauer. The defendants had done their best to slow things down over the years. But things were coming to a close. We were told that a court date had been set for December, and as a result, my sisters and I, along with some of our husbands, had to give our depositions.

I was terrified. Knowing that I was going to be questioned by lawyers for hours and give my account of what had happened, sent me back to some of my most anxious moments—to El Salvador, to Megyn Kelly, to the original investigation where I thought that one wrong word from me and we'd all be taken away from Mom and Pops.

In the days leading up to my deposition I couldn't focus, couldn't eat without feeling nauseous, or sleep without falling into a nightmare. Getting out of bed was too much. My stomach felt like it had been wrapped up tight with razor wire. For years I'd tried to bury so much of the pain. I thought I'd dealt with it. But now it was back, and it was more terrifying than ever.

My deposition lasted seven hours. Every second felt like torture.

When it got to be so much I thought I might scream, I'd excused myself and gone to the bathroom. I'd tried to get rid of the fear and the pain, but all I could do was dry heave over the toilet and try to muffle my screams with a pillow.

When it was over, I hugged the boys and cried in Derick's arms until the room was thick with darkness.

Then, in September, we found out that we were expecting. After everything that had happened with Samuel's birth, I had no idea whether I would even be able to get pregnant again, but there it was, the clear pink line on the test. I was so happy, I was even able to bury the feelings that the deposition had stirred up. Yet the next month I miscarried. It hit me hard. As I grieved the loss of little River Bliss Dillard, I was asking big questions about whether

I'd ever have another baby. Part of me understood that if my body wouldn't carry another baby to term, then so be it. I already had two beautiful, healthy boys, and it was easy to be grateful. But I knew I wanted more babies. I had seen health specialists who had given me a protocol for managing any possible pregnancy, so I wasn't done yet. The desire hung over me like a shadow. I didn't know what to do with it.

Ahead of Josh's trial, Pops had to appear in court. I wasn't there, but Derick heard about it from a family friend and told me it had not gone well. Pops seemed scared and belligerent, indignantly telling the judge, "Are you going to let this happen?" after he'd been asked a question that he didn't want to answer about past abuse and the release of information. It hadn't gone down well, and Pops had earned himself a warning from the judge—who happened to be the same guy who was scheduled to hear the case that my sisters and I were bringing.

It was not a good start.

Then, in November, just as I was preparing myself for the fact that Josh's jury trial was about to begin, the unexpected happened. We got pregnant again.

I was on the prosecution's witness list, which meant that I was supposed to avoid reading about the trial. It wasn't easy. Josh's long fall from grace was national news, and at times it seemed like nothing else was going on in the world. I heard from Derick that there were paparazzi outside the courtroom and outside the Big House. The days were long, but I was glad to be spending them quietly at home, with my blinds shut just in case cameras showed up, just hanging with my boys and praying for the health of the new life growing inside me.

At other times, I thought about Josh. I'd been told that I could receive a call at any point and be required to testify against him in court the next day. That was a sobering thought—a little terrifying at times—but I was willing to do it. I had thought about what Josh had done and reached a clear conclusion. After years and years of following the family line and trusting Pops when he said that things were better dealt with within the family, I wanted something different to happen. I wanted to know the truth. I wanted the evidence to come out. And I wanted Josh to be put away for a very long time.

I felt anger at what he'd done—so much anger it burned. He had hurt innocent children by his actions, and then continued to avoid responsibility.

I felt sad, too. Sad that Josh had become such a monster, sad that even with all the chances Josh had been given to change, he had thrown them away as he continued down a dark, terrible road. Like the rest of the world, I was finally able to see my eldest brother for what he was—a man unable to control himself, totally detached from the reality of how deeply he was hurting others.

The more I thought, the more I realized how much I missed my innocent childhood. The days when we used to just run around and play, picking fruit from the trees that filled our yard. Back when there were just eight of us kids, and to me our little garden felt like Eden. But like that first paradise, sin got in. Evil had spread. The innocence was broken.

The trial brought up everything from the past, as news stories resurfaced the abuse. I felt plagued by this, humiliated just like before. But it was different this time. I had a stronger support system of friends. I was learning how to be vulnerable with them about family, and I knew for my own mental health that I couldn't live in isolation this time around. And in return, for the first time ever, I felt overwhelmingly supported.

Friends checked in on me and let me know they were praying. They sent coffee or ordered dinner for my family when I was feeling drained by my pregnancy and didn't have the energy to do anything. It didn't make the problems go away, but it did give me the strength to press on.

And it wasn't just my friends. Some of my siblings started to reach out. For the first time it was clear that some of them were beginning to be skeptical of the narrative they'd been hearing at home. As they looked for themselves at the Duggar family spectacle, they started to ask their own questions.

I hated to be walking through such a painful experience again, and I hated that it had dragged my entire extended family in too, but I was thankful that I could look back and notice the growth, the positive changes in some areas of my relationships and in myself. And that gave me more hope for the future.

Toward the end of the trial, I was told that I was no longer going to be needed to testify. The prosecution had presented all that they needed to present, and my testimony was no longer necessary. I exhaled with relief. Probably cried a little too, especially when Derick got home from the trial that night.

"What are you going to do?" he asked. Being off the witness list meant I was free to visit the court. "Are you going to come?"

I wrestled with it a bit before making a decision.

It was almost impossible to separate the pregnancy nausea from anxiety nausea, and as I walked into the courtroom and sat quietly on the bench beside Derick, I had to take a moment to catch my breath and keep my head from spinning.

When I was able to look up, it hit me how strange it all was.

Josh was sitting with his legal team, looking like he was facing nothing more serious than a parking violation.

There were the family members—Pops; Jessa; Joy and her husband, Austin; Jason; Justin and his wife, Claire; as well as Josh's wife, Anna. They all looked like they were attending a funeral. They were pale. Exhausted. Beaten.

Then there were the journalists, outnumbering everyone else. They were watching all of us, studying and analyzing our every move. I'd never been in a room where I'd felt so claustrophobic. Never felt the urge to run quite so strong within me.

But I didn't run. I stayed and listened to the summing up from both sides. More than once I squeezed Derick's hand. Three from me. Four from him.

Before this latest scandal, there was a part of me that hoped Josh would change, or that at least he might actually want to change.

But as the truth about his actions had emerged, I had become concerned for who else might become a casualty if he was allowed to continue on as he was in the world. It was becoming increasingly clear that the safest place for Josh, and those around him, was prison.

In the past, he had apologized for looking at adult porn. Now that he had walked into deeper and darker sins, he seemed to grow *less* remorseful. He never admitted the crimes he most recently committed, never expressed any guilt or remorse. Maybe he was actually worried this time about the very real potential consequences that faced him. I don't know.

But the whole thing made me feel sick to my core.

I decided against going back to court the next—and final—day. I'd seen enough on that one day, heard enough of the evidence, talked with enough people to not feel the need to return. Besides, I was exhausted, and didn't want to do anything to jeopardize the baby.

But Derick was there for the verdict. And soon after the verdict was handed down, he called me.

"They found him guilty," he said, but I'd been keeping up with the news from my phone, and I already knew.

For a moment I didn't know what to say. After so many words, so many secrets and so many lies, it was hard to put what I felt into syllables. In the end, all I could manage was, "I think they got it right."

Later, Derick and I sat at a laptop and started to type. We wanted to put a statement out on our family blog, and we wanted to do it quickly.

I knew exactly how I wanted it to start, and Derick watched as I typed.

Today was difficult for our family.

Our hearts go out to the victims of child abuse or any kind of exploitation.

After that, I hit a block. I tried a few different lines, but they just looked all wrong on the screen.

"What do you want people to know?" Derick asked.

I closed my eyes.

"That we have been lied to so much. But that finally, today, we got the truth."

A Photo

"Just be careful, Jill."

I sat, exhaled slowly, and let my mind drift to the baby that was bursting to get out of my belly, and the birth that my calendar told me was likely still a month away. Instinct told me to block out the voice of the person talking to me, to ignore it and discount their warnings. But I didn't want to. I wanted to hear what they had to say.

It wasn't a midwife I was talking with, or an OB-GYN, and we weren't in a hospital room or medical office. We were in a coffee shop. The person sitting opposite, offering me advice, was an old friend from back in the days when Sweet Jilly Muffin thought that Mr. Gothard could do no wrong.

"All I'm saying . . ." My friend paused, searching for the words. Maybe she thought I was a minefield. One wrong word and I'd take us both out. But I wasn't on edge, and I wasn't feeling too triggered by this long discussion about my family. It was okay, and I tried to communicate that with my smile.

"All I'm saying, Jill, is don't go throwing the baby out with the bathwater. I owe a lot to your parents. They're good people."

"I know."

Ever since we'd started talking publicly about our decision to put a little distance between us and the family, this kind of conversation was a regular feature in my life. I must have had it twenty other times with twenty different people. But I appreciated it. Or, at least, I'd learned to appreciate it. I'd learned to really listen to what they were saying and the heart behind it. To do that, I had learned to tune out the old echoes of fear and the guilt that had shouted at me for so long.

I'd had other conversations too. Some people—like the father whose child was engaged to be married to one of my siblings—had told me they'd wanted to hear my side of the story. He'd told me that he didn't believe some of the things he'd heard about Derick and me, and he wanted to listen. We'd talked for three hours, and he said it helped him feel more confident about how he could support his child when they finally married into the Duggar family.

Every time I find myself talking with someone who is curious about my family, especially when it's someone who shares an IBLP background, I ask myself some questions. How much truth can they handle? How much truth do they need? Do they actually seem genuinely interested in knowing more or do they seem combative? Will my conversation be beneficial for them in trying to help them figure things out?

Growing up Duggar, there are so many things that I'm grateful for. We had space and freedom and parents who were patient and kind. I read a comment once that criticized Mom and Pops for using their kids as child labor to build their house. That couldn't be further from the truth. I loved being taught how to use a drill or how to lay tile and then being given the trust to go ahead and get on with the job. Mom and Pops didn't treat us as slaves when we were building the Big House, they treated us as co-workers, worthy of respect and praise. And when the job was finished and we got to move in, all of us who were old enough to walk, talk, and at the very least hold a paintbrush, could point to parts of our home and say, "I did that." It gave us a sense of purpose and created within us an even deeper bond that held us together.

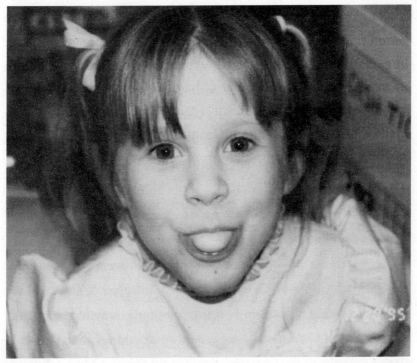

Jilly Muffin, December 1995

I am grateful for the way Mom and Pops taught us how to treat each other. When you have that many kids living and learning together under one roof, you can't be a micromanager, refereeing all their arguments and disagreements. You have to teach them how to get along, and Mom in particular was so good at that. She was always encouraging us to think about what the other person was feeling, to empathize and see things from their perspective. And one of the greatest compliments you could ever give Pops was to tell him that you were impressed by how well we all got along.

"They're best friends," he'd say, his eyes dancing with delight. And he was right. We didn't see the little ones as annoying and we weren't fighting for our parents' attention. We loved each other, and we knew that we were loved in return.

Mom and Pops made time for us individually as well. Whenever either of them was running an errand, they'd take one or two of us along for the ride. We'd often get a dollar to spend in whatever store we were visiting, and they both would make us feel special. We were never in any doubt about the fact that their marriage was their priority, but it was just as clear that they both loved every one of us. For all the times growing up that I heard the phrase "children are a blessing," I never once doubted it. Mom and Pops lived it out loud. They loved us, and they never ceased to take an opportunity to show us that love in action.

I guess things changed with the show. But it's not difficult for me to look back on those days with gratitude. Thanks to the show, we ate well, lived in a beautifully furnished house, traveled the world, and got to feel like we had a sense of purpose and calling as we dedicated ourselves to the ministry. It's one thing to give a kid a drill and

Jill, Jana, and John, early 1990s

show them how to put rivets in a partition wall, it's a whole other level for a kid to have those parents invite them in to share the God-given task of telling the world about how great it is to grow up in a Christian home.

So, yes, I am grateful.

But I am also realistic. There is much that I can look back on and smile, but I picked up some wounds along the way. It's like roses and thorns, justice and grace. You can recognize the beauty and happy parts of your story while also recognizing the more difficult parts. The two *can* coexist. The highs aren't automatically erased or invalidated by the lows.

Ray must have been able to see it the moment we sat down to talk with him. We'd originally gone to him with a plan to restart the mediation process with Mom and Pops, but Ray gently helped us to see that the last thing we needed was a quick fix.

"I'm Muscogee Creek," he said, midway through our first session, "so I'm going to talk about arrows."

"Um, okay," we said, not really knowing what else to say.

"You've been in a battle for a long time. You've taken a lot of arrows, and there are more coming. Occasionally, back in the day, when someone would get shot with an arrow, the arrowhead might get lost inside them, and anytime that area got bumped it would be extremely painful. You've got a lot of different wounds on you. Some are old, some are new. And I don't think many of those wounds have healed right."

The room stopped. My breath grew shallow. Cry or run, I didn't know what I wanted to do. So I just sat and listened.

"That's why it hurts so bad so much of the time, Jill. Even when people do the slightest thing—maybe Derick says or does something dumb—but it bumps one of those arrowheads and triggers all that old pain. So, no, you don't need a mediation meeting with your parents right now. You don't need to go back into battle. You need to heal. Really heal."

It took years for us to put the puzzle pieces together, years for us to start to identify the reasons why things felt like they did. It took a lot of talking with Mr. McIntosh, a lot of talking with each other, and a lot of getting things wrong more often than we got things right. We had to learn how to talk to each other—becoming attuned—and I in particular had to learn how to trust people. Decades of fear and paranoia didn't unravel overnight.

Things like Josh's trial and my deposition were tough, sending me spiraling back into the panic and the fear. At times, even today, there are periods where it feels like the old pressures come at me in waves and I have to work hard to keep the weight off my shoulders. But slowly, gradually, we have started to find a route away from the pain. The wounds are still there, but the scar tissue is growing thicker.

In the same way that we'd thought that mediation was going to be our way to the finish line with Mom and Pops, I'd hoped that the lawsuit against the City of Springdale, Arkansas; Washington County, Arkansas; Kathy O'Kelley; Ernest Cate; Rick Hoyt; *In Touch* magazine and its parent company Bauer; and anyone else involved behind the scenes would bring closure and healing to that most painful part of my life.

It didn't. At least, not in the way that I'd hoped.

Right from the beginning we knew the law was on our side. But what started out as a winnable case—so winnable that the law firm took it on contingency, putting millions of dollars into litigation that spanned five years—suddenly became weak once my brother appeared in court.

Our case was derailed by everything that happened with Josh. The fact that we were due to appear in the same court, before the same judge, likely with jurors drawn from the same jury pool, meant that we were tied to him. It was another painful twist of the knife to be linked to our abuser like this, but there was nothing we could do. After Josh's trial revealed the continued secrecy in our family and the lack of acknowledgment of wrongdoing, the judge and everyone around grew skeptical of anything to do with the Duggars. They lumped us all together, and despite the fact that our case was strong, we could feel the tide turning against us. Even though we were suing those who the judge agreed had illegally released the reports of our abuse and then exploited us as victims of child sexual abuse, in many people's eyes the court had already declared who the real culprit was—Josh.

In February 2022, my phone pinged a local news alert as I simultaneously received media requests for comment.

The judge had dismissed our case. When the judge released his opinion, he made it crystal clear that the graphic reports of child sexual abuse victims were illegally released. He wrote that what the defendants did was "profoundly wrong" and that "[i]f the question is whether Defendants were ignorant of the law or grossly negligent in its application, the answer is: Absolutely." He went on to say that "Arkansas FOIA [Freedom of Information Act] is not all-inclusive," and that in our case "all individual Defendants were seemingly ignorant of the privacy rights Arkansas affords to sexual assault victims and to the families that are identified as 'in need of services.'" He further stated that "neither report should have been released" due to the "clear and unambiguous" laws the officials broke: "AR Code § 16-90-1104(b)" and the Child Maltreatment Act "Ark. Code Ann. § 12-18-104(a)." But even though I felt somewhat vindicated since the judge recognized that the reports had been illegally released and that none of this should have ever happened, it still wasn't much consolation. The officials were granted "immunity" because of their status. The lasting, personal damage had been done. I had been identified and re-traumatized, had sought legal recourse, but was now collateral damage in a seemingly unchecked system. And the thought of making more appeals wasn't much good either, because we'd only get tied up with the ongoing circus and court proceedings surrounding Josh. We had lost. It was all over.

Some people were supportive. Others said we were blaming the wrong people, that it was all Mom and Pops' fault. I could feel another wave of anxiety and fear about to wash over me, but I held tight to some of the most powerful advice that Mr. McIntosh had given Derick and me:

"Sometimes you have to be okay with other people not being okay with you. And you have to be okay with you not being okay too."

I had always struggled in that area. I grew up believing subconsciously that whenever there was any bad feeling, it was up to me to do what I could to fix it. It worked when my world began and ended with the Big House, but not anymore. There was just no way of changing the way that millions of people saw me. If they disapproved and didn't like what I'd done, I had to be okay with that.

With time, I was able to see that even though our lawsuit was thrown out, our fight for justice had left a positive legacy for us both. It was what drove Derick to enroll in law school, and what inspired him to take on his first job after graduation as an assistant district attorney in Oklahoma. Today, he is able to fight for victims' rights in ways that neither of us were able to do before. Every week he strives to protect victims from being blamed, shamed, and bullied into silence.

Only now can I look back and see things clearly, like the way IBLP fostered a culture of manipulation and abuse, the fact that Pops eventually put the show above his children, or the toll it took on my own mental health.

I also see Mom more clearly today. I see the myriad ways she cared for us when we were growing up, the sacrifices she made, and the depth of her love for people. I love her, respect her, and look up to her. She is the first person I call whenever I have a question about our baby's health, and I love that we can still connect that way no matter what family drama is occurring.

But I miss her too. I miss the ease of communication we used to have. I miss it so much that there are times I almost wonder if it would be better to go back to the way things were, when Derick and I were happy to fall into line and silence our questions. Wouldn't it be good to be free from all this struggle and heartache? Is ignorance really bliss? I know the answer is no, just like I know that I must at times sacrifice a degree of closeness in my relationship with Mom. And I also know that any time I want to get together there's a chance emotions will get stirred up again. It's all part of the cost that we count these days, and I pray this troubled season won't last. I believe there are better days ahead.

I remember Pops clearly too. My dad always had a great capacity for love and for fun, and though he wasn't quite as emotionally in tune as Mom, he was still very caring, and I could still have deep conversations way into my teens. I never doubted that he loved us kids, and never doubted that he loved Mom either. He would often tell my mom not to worry about keeping everything looking just perfect at home. To him, what mattered most was that us children got what we needed and Mom was able to take good care of us.

Pops made life fun. He could transform a family bike ride or a night spent camping out in the front yard into a real adventure. He was there for us, and even when he was picking up a zillion

Popsicle wrappers that we'd left in the yard on a summer's day and threatening to ban us from having Popsicles for a while, we knew he wouldn't be too hard on us. He struck a good balance. He wanted us to have fun, and he made sure that we did. I loved him, and still do. It's just that the show and time seemed to have changed things.

Getting out cost us, but it was worth it. It was worth it to find freedom from the guilt and the fear. It was worth it to learn how to think for myself about what I really believed about everything from God and the Bible to how many kids we should have and how they should be educated. It was worth it to discover that standing up for myself or others isn't a sin or an act of disobedience. It's a mark of freedom, of self-respect, of dignity. In learning to treat myself more kindly, I am discovering that it's possible to do the same for others as well.

In May 2022, not long after Josh had been sentenced to serve twelve and a half years in prison, I let myself start to think about the upcoming birth. The little one that had been growing inside me since November wasn't so little anymore, and at first my mind returned to my previous labors and deliveries with Israel and Samuel. I knew it would be different, and hopefully less stressful this time with a slightly early, planned C-section, but there were still so many unknowns. Memories of the pain, the fear, the risk were still fresh, but I did not want to let them take hold of me. I wanted to spend my final weeks of pregnancy looking forward, not back.

We were at home when I asked Derick the question that had been brewing within me for days. "How do you feel about my mom being at the birth? Maybe she could help out here when I get home, as well."

Derick smiled. "That would be good. She's been at the others."

My next question came out before I could help it. "What about Pops?"

"I don't know. Do we want him to meet the baby here? Would a neutral location be better?"

We left the discussion about Pops for another day, but never really got around to it.

When I started dilating and had to have the baby before my scheduled C-section date, Mom came straight over. She was great, as any woman would be who has given birth more than nineteen times (including losses) and been present at the birth of most of her thirty-plus grandchildren. Cathy and my friend Sierra came to wait with the boys, and in spite of the regular but slightly earlier than planned C-section, and the background fear that my uterus might rupture again, I was able to exhale just a little knowing that my family was there with me. There were no cameras, but I was still a Duggar.

Frederick "Freddy" Dillard came into this world with a shout, and my uterus held up just fine. He had to spend a few days in the NICU since he was a bit early, but there was nothing that any-body was worried about. When he was finally ready to come home, Mom rode in the car with me and Freddy. She'd been amazing all through the delivery, as well as after it, helping me with the baby, night feedings, and tending to my every need as I recovered from the C-section. We were able to connect in ways we'd not connected for years, and I was grateful for this unexpected gift.

When we got back to our house, Mom checked her phone.

"It's Pops," she said. "He's going to come get me."

Her voice trailed off. She looked concerned. I glanced at Derick. He looked at me. We both knew the answer to the question that Mom hadn't asked.

"Okay," I said.

"You should tell Pops to come inside so he can meet Freddy," said Derick warmly.

When Pops arrived a half hour later, he looked around slowly, like he was taking it all in. We'd moved houses a month earlier, and this was his first time over. He'd never been to our previous place either, and we'd lived there for three years, so this was all new to him. He looked content, but like he was quickly having to redraw a map of how Derick and I lived.

I needed to redraw my map too. In previous years, I'd seen him a few times at family events—weddings, funerals, court cases—but never somewhere this quiet, this private. He looked different. A little older, perhaps. The way he carried himself, there wasn't the same sense of authority and power than he'd once had.

As soon as Pops saw baby Freddy, his expression changed. His eyes found their old sparkle, his smile fired up again. Of all the many different parts to him—Head of the Duggar Household, CEO of Mad Family Inc, politician, public figure—it was plain old Grandpa Duggar who I found the easiest to love. There was nothing complex there, nothing to worry about. Just a man taking delight in the precious baby that his daughter had just brought into the world.

For a long time we all just stood and smiled, Pops looking at Freddy, us looking at Pops.

"Jill, Derick," Mom said eventually. "Would y'all mind if Pops held Freddy?"

"Sure," I said. "We should get a photo, too."

Jim Bob and Michelle with baby Freddy, July 2022

AUTHOR'S NOTE

⎯⎯∞∞⎯⎯

What this book is not . . .

This book is not a letter to my family as part of the reconciliation process. I also didn't write this book to shame my family or just to try and get their attention. We will continue to work through matters with family independent of this book with the desired ultimate goal of healthy relationships, Lord willing. We understand that no family is perfect and that you can recognize the beauty in your story while still acknowledging the difficult parts and even setting boundaries. It shouldn't make you unloving. It's like roses and thorns, the two can coexist, and I do love my family. The highs aren't invalidated by the lows and vice versa. Everyone's story will look different. Just because some problems weren't intentional, or one story isn't as bad as the next person's, shouldn't invalidate the real problems or minimize the story.

And the degree to which we felt this book needed to be written, was the degree to which we felt like voices were still being silenced and real harm was continuing to be done by not telling it.

ACKNOWLEDGMENTS

"Speak truth even if your voice shakes."
—Source Unknown

Like the Old Testament story of the support provided to Moses by Aaron and Hur when they helped hold his arms up to ensure a successful battle for Israel, I have felt so supported in many ways on this book writing journey.

I want to thank our pastor, friends, and family who have supported us either quietly or openly as we have lived our story and then started the process to tell it in book form.

I'm grateful to our agent, Anthony Mattero, and his team at Creative Artists Agency who believed in us and have been super helpful in walking us through the whole book process.

Thanks also to the amazing team at Gallery Books and Simon & Schuster: Natasha Simons, Mia Robertson, Lauren Carr, and Anabel Jimenez.

Photographer Christopher Patey and his assistant, Jack, were so gracious to come to our home and shoot around our toy-scattered living room, allowing for frequent breaks to care for our baby.

Thanks to my sweet friend and owner of BLONDE salon, Michelle Gamboa, who came to do my hair and makeup on cover shoot day but was also totally there to support me and jumped in to help with the baby, too.

A huge thanks to our writer, Craig Borlase. From the time we received his bio to when he crossed the pond from Britain to help us start this process, our trust and confidence in him only grew. He embodies what it means to walk a mile in someone's shoes as he used his therapist-like gift of listening (for hours and days!) and then compiled and helped us put our often-complicated story into words. His own life experiences and previous work only added to the care and attention he showed us in the more sensitive parts of our story. We couldn't be more grateful for Craig. The Yorkshire tea, Curly Wurlys, and help with getting the London accent right were added bonuses.

We are so thankful for our therapist, Mr. Raymond McIntosh, who for countless hours has helped us process the highs and lows of our story. Like a guide, Mr. McIntosh gave us so many tools we didn't know we needed when we needed them most. He pointed us back to Jesus and helped us find our voice. We are forever grateful for his help and support! He was an answer to our prayers. Everyone needs a therapist like Mr. McIntosh!

Our sons, Israel, Samuel and Frederick, who gave us some of the greatest motivation to keep going.

My husband, Derick Dillard, who has walked through the fire and every therapy session with me and been my greatest support, advocate, and coffee and sushi supplier. Babe, without you I wouldn't have found the strength to face my giants, count the cost, or find my voice. It's been a journey, but there's nobody I'd rather live it with than you! ILYSM!

My Lord and Savior, Jesus Christ, who I owe my life to, who has sustained us through it all, and who promises to never leave us or forsake us through the rest of our journey!